CALM THE CHAOS

Cognitive Behavioral Therapy workbook for adults to cure depression, and anxiety and create positive thoughts

ANGELA WADE

SPECIAL BONUS!

Want this bonus book for free?

Get unlimited access to this and all of my new books by joining the Fan Base!

Scan with your camera to join!

CONTENTS

INTRODUCTION

Many of us live in continual fear of failure, which is due, in part, to popular ideals about health and success, as well as demands to adhere to these norms. We all have opinions about what it means to be smart, successful, outgoing, and ambitious. People with mental illnesses, on the other hand, are unfairly stigmatized and are rarely thought of in this light – that they can be intelligent, funny, and successful – particularly when they are in and out of psychiatric hospitals, over-medicating, or have highly stigmatizing illnesses like psychosis, autism, bipolar disorder, and borderline personality disorder, or severe alcohol and drug addiction.

This book is intended to help you grow in self-awareness and self-compassion. As you work your way through these chapters, you will begin to feel more self-assured and confident, no longer powerless but clear-headed and composed. These actionable steps and guidelines will help you start on an exhilarating new journey of self-discovery.

CHAPTER 1

INTRODUCTION TO MENTAL HEALTH

What do we mean when we say mental health and illness? What does it mean to be mentally healthy or ill? What first comes to mind when we think about mental health? What is the public's perception of people with mental illnesses, and how they are depicted in the media? Are these representations accurate?

People with mental illnesses are frequently accused of exhibiting strange, potentially deviant conduct. What, on the other hand, distinguishes normal from deviant behavior? Are the lines between what's acceptable and what's not always clear?

Millions of individuals are affected and diagnosed with mental illnesses every year, which has significant repercussions on their social, physical, economic, and spiritual health and well-being. Children, adolescents, adults, families, and entire communities can all be affected by mental illness. According to the National Alliance on Mental Illness, one out of every five adults and one out of every six children suffers from mental illness each year, resulting in high rates of emergency room visits, psychiatric hospitalization, learning and behavior issues, homelessness, disability, and unemployment or under-employment.

Research has found that those who have struggled with depression, anxiety, schizophrenia, bipolar disorder, trauma, or PTSD, on the other hand, frequently have tremendous strengths hidden by an exclusive emphasis on flaws, deficiencies, mental health symptoms, and disruptions.

Stigma, prejudice, and unfavorable or biased ideas and assumptions about people with mental illness are frequently reflected and reinforced by social standards, media depictions, and mainstream perspectives on mental health (for example, that they are dangerous, sick, and emotionally unstable). Our perspectives on mental disease evolve over time. At one point, a behavior may be considered abnormal or suggestive of a psychiatric disorder (for example, psychotic symptoms commonly associated with schizophrenia, such as paranoia). At another point, it may be considered normal and appropriate behavior (e.g., healthy paranoia, for example, checking to make sure your door is locked either because there have been robberies and break-ins in your neighborhood or perhaps you are nervous from binging on scary movies from your favorite streaming service).

Furthermore, what constitutes abnormal depends on cultural beliefs, norms, values, religion, and family systems. People's ideas on truth, science, and medicine, and their trust in established healthcare systems and practices, including prescription drugs or, by comparison, alternative (complementary) treatments and rituals, also influence their views.

Experts also disagree on what causes mental health issues and what people can do to enhance their physical and psychological health. These notions have an impact on how mental health clinicians engage with people who are experiencing psychological distress and seek therapy.

Cognitive psychologists, for example, believe that mental disease stems from cognitive dysfunction. They highlight terms like cognitive (thinking) distortions to explain how people acquire mental health issues as a result of poor thinking habits and flawed belief systems.

Consider the following example of how one's ideas might lead to mental anguish. You are not alone if you suffer from depression. Depression is one of the most prevalent mental health diseases we see in healthcare, and studies have shown that depression has a reasonably high incidence rate in the general population. In other words, most individuals have been sad or melancholy at some point in their lives, whether or not they have been diagnosed with clinical depression. Others, such as family, friends, teachers, religious personnel, coworkers, and healthcare providers, were called upon in certain circumstances.

According to cognitive scientists, sadness drives people to think in ways that, if left unchecked or unchallenged, could be harmful. Depression is thought to be a manifestation of mental disorders, particularly negative (maladaptive) thinking, which affects motivation, mood, self-esteem, perceived competency, decision-making, happiness, and hope.

Introduction to Cognitive Restructuring

Individuals who have suffered depression have reported the following cognitive distortions:

Nobody cares for me. I just don't feel like I'm supposed to be here. I'm a loser.
My situation will never improve.
I should've realized I wasn't going to get the job.

It's easy to understand how this kind of thinking might skew people's perceptions of themselves and the world. Individuals with depression process information through a depressive lens, focusing on the negative, discounting positive experiences, or convincing themselves that positive moments are fleeting and rare, most likely due to chance, and thus insufficient to help them reframe their depressive belief systems, which may be more comfortable and familiar.

Cognitive restructuring, which is intrinsically related to cognitive therapy treatment, is the process of shifting our thinking from negative to more adaptive and rational perspectives. You may be acquainted with terminology like automatic thoughts or assumptions, reframing or learning to see things differently, erroneous beliefs, biased thinking, and evidence-based ideas to express this and other cognitive concepts.

We put our ideas through tests, such as analyzing evidence for and against a belief or hypothesis, but we don't test them for truth or objectivity. Consider the thought tasks below for each distortion to see how cognitive therapists may help people with depression improve and learn to see the world more objectively.

Nobody cares for me. I just don't feel like I'm supposed to be here.

What evidence do you have that no one likes you? How do you determine whether or not people like you? What are your standards? Is it true that if one person dislikes you, everyone dislikes you? Is it reasonable to want everyone to like you? What does it signify if someone disapproves of you? Is it necessary for it to indicate something negative about you, or may we consider it in a different light? Isn't it feasible, for example, that they despise themselves? That they despise a lot of people, implying that it's about them rather than you?

I'm a loser — are you always a loser?

What do you mean when you say "failure"? Can we take a look at occasions when you didn't fail? How would you help someone you care about, such as a family member or a friend, think differently if they told you they were a failure? Some individuals feel that failure is a necessary component of success. How may this apply to you? Let's think of a time when you felt successful.

My situation will never improve.

How did you figure that out? What are your hopes and dreams? Are they plausible? Is it possible to truly know what the future holds? Isn't it possible that things will improve for you? What changes can you make to go to a better (or different) place? When you start to believe that things aren't going to get any better, what can you say to yourself? Maybe you might remind yourself that you're getting help and making progress. Perhaps we can shift our perceptions of what it means to improve — maybe getting well involves talking to someone like you are right now, taking one day at a time, being kind and nonjudgmental to yourself, and remembering that life is always changing. If you believe that life will not improve, you will reaffirm that belief despite evidence to the contrary.

I should've realized I wasn't going to get the job.

You had no way of knowing. Are you relying on emotional reasoning rather than rational reasoning in this situation? Is there a chance that something better or different is still out there for you to discover? Could it be that, despite your desire for this career, the universe is sending you a sign that this isn't your ideal fit? Even if we don't realize it at the time, the things we want aren't always the greatest for us. Can we make use of this chance to work on correcting cognitive distortions?

The cognitive approach to mental health emphasizes ideas, assumptions, and maladaptive thoughts that, if left unquestioned, evolve into thinking habits, many of which are negative. We can change for the better. It all starts with believing in new possibilities. Cognitive psychology has grown in popularity because of its scientific foundations and documented research support.

Cognitive techniques strive to empower people by fostering independence and self-control, particularly in areas of life that can be altered, such as our underlying beliefs and assumptions, and our interpretations of events, particularly stressful and traumatic situations. According to cognitive theorists, people are not characterized by a diagnostic category or sickness. Thoughts are the basis of mental health issues, and they may be changed to increase self-awareness, quality of life, interpersonal connections, and problem-solving.

Understanding mental health, adopting self-help tactics, and reframing notions about what distinguishes normal and abnormal behavior are all topics covered in this book. Mental disease is not a static entity or a category that exists indefinitely. People have good days and bad days, and mental health symptoms fluctuate based on a variety of circumstances, including the environment, stress, coping, social support, and, most importantly, self-care routines. This book will be a helpful resource for readers interested in learning more about healthy habits for excellent health and different strategies from Cognitive Behavioral Therapy used for a wide range of audiences and situations.

We believe that by doing so, the method would provide readers with various viewpoints on mental health and enlighten them on how we have come to define well-being from different angles, including strengths and resiliencies.

Suffering may be seen in a variety of ways, such as an experience, a symptom, or, by comparison, as a precursor to personal growth and development.

We also have our own cognitive biases and assumptions, such as the fact that we may become accustomed to treating particular patients since "we've treated many patients like that previously..." Patients' distinctive features, like their wants, goals and ambitions, communication style, intersubjective experiences, and strengths, may be overlooked when we describe them by their symptoms. Furthermore, our perspectives, experiences, and therapeutic methods and procedures as healthcare practitioners differ.

Consider the example of cognitive theories that place higher importance on present-focused thinking rather than traumatic childhood events, such as ongoing disagreements with caregivers that might lead to recurrent relationship issues in adulthood.

Sigmund Freud popularized the terms id, ego, superego, and defense mechanisms, referring to unconscious psychological processes that help reduce our experiences of stress, anxiety, and fear, such as denying that a problem exists or displacing our feelings of anger and frustration on others regardless of the circumstances. You may have experienced displacement if you were having a horrible day and suddenly yelled at a loved one for no apparent cause. Displacement is supposedly beyond our immediate knowledge and control. Happiness, on the other hand, can be contagious.

Why use a cognitive behavioral approach in the first place?

Traditionally, dealing with mental diseases was inspired by the medical paradigm, which saw mental illnesses as chronic, with permanent neuropathological brain alterations and information processing deficiencies. People with mental diseases saw themselves adversely as a result of this negative approach, which frequently created the stigma that they were different from others. Other issues, such as loneliness and low self-esteem, might arise as a result. Those with serious mental diseases frequently have low self-esteem, poor quality of life, and poor psychosocial functioning, which is unsurprising. Rather than approaching mental illnesses through the traditional medical model, which focuses on pathology, problems, weaknesses, and failures in people, the cognitive-behavioral approach allows various aspects of a person's life with a mental illness to be acknowledged and then changed to help them overcome their problem.

The cognitive behavioral method focuses on an individual's ideas and actions, assisting them in managing their difficulties by altering their thinking and behavior. The focus is on the person's beliefs and activities rather than their flaws, symptoms, or issues. Mental illness is no longer regarded as a taboo subject but rather as a natural part of life. Individuals' ideas, actions, and talents are theorized and analyzed, and therapy aims to build on these strengths, leading to the accomplishment of desired outcomes.

Cognitive therapy, behavioral therapy, and mindfulness-based treatments are the three core components of the cognitive behavioral approach.

Cognitive therapy focuses on thinking patterns as the source of negative emotional and behavioral actions. In this view, inadequate or exaggerated biases in thinking produce and sustain mental health problems. Identifying dysfunctional or distorted habits and learning to respond to them with more reality-based ideas is the crucial remedy here. Consequently, there are fewer emotional disorders and more effective behavioral patterns.

Behavioral treatment emphasizes behavior as the most important factor influencing dysfunctional psychological processes. Issues are addressed, and problematic behaviors are recognized in behavioral therapy. The central mechanism of change in behavioral therapy is facilitating the acquisition and application of beneficial behaviors to replace dysfunctional or ineffective behaviors. This might include modeling and teaching new behaviors, increasing exposure to previously avoided stimuli, and enhancing rewarding behavior.

Mindfulness-based treatments are a newer addition to cognitive behavioral therapy. Mindfulness is a type of meditation that involves focusing on and nonjudgmental attention to the work at hand. Mindfulness treatment was developed to help people improve the spiritual training of the mind. More recently, researchers have employed some of its most successful components to treat anxiety, depression, bipolar disorder, PTSD, OCD, ADHD, and chronic pain. Mindfulness-based cognitive behavioral treatments are effective therapeutic alternatives. In recent research, mindfulness for anxiety and depression has been demonstrated to be considerably more beneficial than standard treatments such as talk therapy.

CHAPTER 2

ANXIETY AND STRESS

Research and Overview

Stress is one way our bodies let us know that something is wrong that we need to mend or rectify. It is necessary for our existence and health. Still, this warning system might go off for no apparent reason, and we become physically and emotionally tense in order to combat an issue when the underlying problem is in our heads. The inability to tell the difference between actual and beneficial stress, harmful worry, and dread is common. But how can you be certain that a certain circumstance won't result in a problem? The truth is you can't. We may, however, learn to distinguish excessive responses, such as being afraid in an elevator. Some people, on the other hand, underreact to a circumstance. They either underestimate or deny the circumstance, such as never preparing for work—both tendencies lead to bad conduct; exaggerating and underestimating the threat leads to poor behavior.

The reality is that we are all anxious at some point in our lives. Each of us has our own level of complexity. Various terms like nervous, concerned, terrified, insecure, panicked, and so on may be used to characterize it. The most prevalent signs of mental diseases are stress and worry.

Internal processes (perception, interpretation of the event, learning, adaptation, or coping mechanisms), emotional reactions (our feelings), and other behavioral-bodily reactions are all included in the definitions: (1) the event requires some change (external or mental; real or imaginary), (2) internal processes (perception, interpretation of the event, learning, adaptation, or coping mechanisms), (3) emotional reactions (our feelings), and (4) other behavioral-bodily reactions (nervousness, sweating, high blood pressure, and other medical conditions). Stress is defined as the mental and bodily responses to a potentially dangerous circumstance.

Fear is linked to stress and can result in panic attacks accompanied by symptoms such as fast breathing, heart palpitations, and a desire to flee the situation. Anxiety, like the other anxiety states, is a distressing condition.

As previously said, these signals help us to deal with situations and achieve our objectives. As a result, warnings must be acknowledged and understood.

Let's start with the second most frequent mental disease after depression, Generalized Anxiety Disorder (GAD). GAD is a long-term condition marked by excessive worry, disruptive anxiety, and tension that lasts at least six months, or even years. It is curable, yet even in wealthy nations, less than 20% of victims receive effective treatment. Hypervigilance, irritability, insomnia, and other bodily symptoms, such as perspiration and heart palpitations, are among the symptoms.

Because anxiety disorders are beneficial, they are difficult to stop, especially when they become chronic. According to research, anxiety is a complicated process rather than a simple conditioned response, a physiological imbalance, or a cognitive mistake. Emotions aren't straightforward; they're always changing and complicated.

Panic disorder, on the other hand, is a mental condition defined by panic episodes, which are the consequence of a complex combination of (1) basic intrinsic biological alarm reactions (emotions), (2) learned psychological coping strategies, and (3) life pressures.

A variety of methods are used to assess stress and anxiety due to their complexity. These include self-ratings, observation by others, psychometric testing, physiological or medical tests, and others. Unfortunately, no measure can be 100 percent accurate since 1. each of us has a unique response to stress, 2. there is no agreement among these measures, and 3. stress and anxiety definitions are so ambiguous that measurements can't describe psychological disorders.

WORKBOOK: OVERCOMING WORRY AND ANXIETY WITH CBT

Overview

Module 1: Overview of anxiety

Module 2: Overview of worrying

Module 3: Beliefs and thoughts

Module 4: Exercises for managing worry and anxiety

Module 1: Overview of Anxiety

Understanding Anxiety

Anxiety is a distressing emotion that everyone encounters from time to time, and it can be experienced in different ways. You may describe it as "nervousness" or "feeling tensed up."

You may also describe it as fear, a highly severe form of anxiety that is usually a reaction to an immediate and specific event. This fear might develop in social circumstances or while thinking about an upcoming social occasion. Thus, we refer to it as "social anxiety." Others have severe fear in response to relatively particular things, such as snakes, heights, or water.

Phobias are the name given to these anxieties. Others may experience a type of fear that feels like "terror," and these are referred to as panic attacks.

General anxiety can continue for long periods – sometimes weeks. You might have thoughts about yourself, others, and the world around you and what is to come in the future.

Anxious people generally think negatively about:

Themselves

- ✓ I cannot cope
- ✓ I am not safe
- ✓ I am going to die

Others

- ✓ I cannot trust people
- ✓ People don't like me
- ✓ People I like will get hurt

The world

- ✓ The world isn't safe
- ✓ The world is a dangerous place

Symptoms of anxiety

- ✓ Do I have symptoms of anxiety?
- ✓ Do you spend a large chunk of your day worrying?

✓ Do you find it difficult to relax?

✓ Do you feel constant nervousness, panic, and stress?

✓ Do you experience frequent somatic symptoms such as tense/sore muscles, shortness of breath, heart palpitations, or upset stomach?

✓ Do you experience difficulty concentrating and have memory problems?

If you answered 'yes' to two or more of the above questions, you may be suffering from anxiety.

Because anxiety is unpleasant, and many of the physical symptoms mimic other serious medical conditions, you may be concerned that you may have a grave health problem. This can make you even more anxious, which creates a cycle of anxiety.

What causes anxiety?

You may feel anxious for several reasons that you might not be aware of at the moment.

Psychological reasons

✓ Negative thoughts about yourself, others, and the world

✓ Early childhood experiences / traumatic events

✓ Modelling anxious behaviors seen in others in your environment. E.g., growing up with an anxious parent.

Social and environmental reasons

✓ Bullying

- ✓ Stress at work
- ✓ Relationship problems
- ✓ Financial problems
- ✓ Expectations

Biological

- ✓ Anxiety disorders run in families.

Module 2: Overview of Worrying

Understanding Worrying

Worrying may be thought of as a self-talk activity in which we speak to ourselves constantly about potential future situations that we are scared of. We mentally replay the incident in our head over and again, imagining what would happen if it happened. Worrying is, therefore, a sort of alertness for any threat, and an effort to solve a problem that has yet to occur.

What Triggers Worrying?

Worrying can be induced by a variety of factors. Some triggers may be more evident and connected to external factors such as: Seeing a specific picture (e.g., on the news), receiving specific information (e.g., on the radio), being placed in a specific setting (e.g., performing a task at work), and others.

Some triggers may be less subtle, such as random ideas or pictures that come to mind out of nowhere. Most of the time, questions that start with the initial "What if..." are a trigger for worry.

Exercise:

What was a recent "what if" thought that came to mind, and what did you do then?

Write down any information, events, internal images, or thoughts that have triggered worry for you.

What Maintains Worrying?

Chronic worriers are frequently troubled by the fact that they appear to spend the majority of their day thinking excessively about various things. They are perplexed as to why this mental activity persists. A worrier's most common question is, "Why do I keep worrying?"

The following are the three things that keep our worrying going.

1. Beliefs

Worriers typically detest the fact that they worry so much but also frequently have positive ideas that worrying is good and helpful. Our positive ideas cause us to worry in the first place. Some examples of positive beliefs include "Worrying helps my problem-solving abilities," "Worrying drives me to action," and "When I worry, I am safe."

Because of this positive view about worrying, when a problem arises that we are concerned about, we draw negative ideas closer.

In addition, worriers may hold negative beliefs about worrying. For example, people may feel, "Worrying is harmful and will drive me crazy" or "I cannot stop worrying". Holding these negative views makes worrying more stressful, causing even more anxiety, and prolonging this process.

2. Attention

People who worry frequently have trouble diverting their attention away from their annoying thoughts in order to focus on their current job, partly because they are unaware they are doing it and partly because they believe it is beneficial to think more about things.

3. Useless Strategies

People who worry frequently try and fail in a variety of unhelpful ways to stop their unpleasant thoughts, including cognitive and behavioral techniques.

Cognitive techniques may include:

- Suppressing their thoughts
- Reasoning
- Distracting their attention
- Positive thinking

Behavioral techniques may include:

- Seeking excessive reassurance from others
- Substance/alcohol abuse
- Checking excessively for information related to their worry.

Cognitive and behavioral techniques such as the above seldom succeed.

How do you try to stop your worries?

_____

_____   _____

_____

_____

Module 3: Beliefs and thoughts

Automatic thinking and beliefs

What you think and the ideas that run through your head have a big impact on how you feel. Consider this for a moment. What kind of thoughts run through your mind while you are feeling good? In contrast, what are your thoughts when you are feeling down?

Patterns of dysfunctional thinking

Automatic thoughts are dysfunctional thoughts that come into your mind without conscious effort. They are plausible and generally distressing, which might affect your emotions and actions. It is critical to remember that thought is not always a fact. You may feel the thoughts that arise in your head, but you must examine them. Knowing the basic patterns that dysfunctional thoughts follow will help you to recognize and challenge them before they affect your mental health.

Here are some examples of automatic thinking:

- ✓ I don't have control over this
- ✓ I will be embarrassed
- ✓ What if I don't get a job?

✓ What if they don't like me?

Here are some examples of dysfunctional thinking:

Emotional reasoning: The practice of considering feelings as though they are facts.

Black and white thinking: When someone is nervous, they typically perceive things as black or white, with nothing in between.

Catastrophizing: People believe anything that has happened is considerably worse than it is.

Labeling: People label themselves negatively.

Neglecting the positives: People disregard the good parts of a situation and focus on the negative.

Personalization: People think everything has something to do with them and blame themselves for no rational reason.

Must statements: People frequently live by a set of rules about what they "must" do and feel and are extremely self-critical if they don't fulfill these expectations.

Overgeneralization: People believe that all future events will follow a similar pattern of one isolated experience, and they tend to dismiss a one-time occurrence as an accident.

Jumping to conclusions: People believe they know what others are thinking.

Challenging your thoughts

Before we start challenging your thoughts, we need to know how much you believe your worrying is uncontrollable. Do you totally and completely believe this? Do you believe this all the time?

Do I have control over my worry? (Circle the percentage that describes the strength of your belief)

0%   10%   20%   30%   40%   50%   60%
       70%   80%   90%   100%

I don't believe   Strongly believe

You must do two things to change your belief that your worry is uncontrollable. To begin, you must confront your beliefs. This entails processing the belief by determining if it's factual and truthful and assessing the information on which you base your belief. Think of yourself as a detective trying to solve the case. Experimenting with the belief will help you determine whether or not worrying is uncontrollable. Can you demonstrate the belief is not true? Then, it means that you can manage your worrying.

Challenging automatic thoughts

By asking the following questions, you may now confront your automatic thoughts. Work your way through the questions below.

Example:

"My professor was supposed to send me the exam results one week ago, and they didn't yet. I must have failed the exam."

Is there any evidence against this thought?

Is there any evidence to support this thought?

Are there any patterns of dysfunctional thinking that you can identify?

What would you say to a friend who is thinking the same thing in a comparable situation?

Is there another way to look at this situation?

Is there a proactive way to deal with this negative automatic thought?

Exercise:

Belief: "My worrying is uncontrollable"	
Evidence for	*Evidence against*
e.g., Since it feels uncontrollable, therefore it must be. [This is not great evidence that you cannot control worrying. Just because you feel it, it doesn't mean it's true.	e.g., I stop worrying when I feel I have worried all day. [My worrying can't be uncontrollable if it doesn't go on forever] e.g., Sometimes, when I am busy doing a task, I do not worry. [If being busy can stop worrying from happening, then it means it can't be uncontrollable]
Your Belief: " "	
Evidence for	*Evidence against*

Module 4: Exercises for Managing Worry and Anxiety

Managing your worry

Anxious people might spend a lot of time worrying, which is only beneficial when it drives you to act. Otherwise, it's just damaging thoughts running in circles. One of the most upsetting things about worry is the feeling that you have no control over it. Learning to control how much you worry can help you feel less anxious. Setting aside some time to worry consciously is one method to accomplish this. It may give you a feeling of control in your worrying so that you will not feel overwhelmed in other situations.

Exercise:

1) Establish a 10 to 15-minute worry time every day.

2) During the day, try not to think about your problems and remind yourself that you have already scheduled worry time.

3) When worry time approaches, start timing yourself so it doesn't last more than 15 minutes.

4) Allow yourself to worry during this time. Don't try to fight your worry and concentrate solely on the process.

5) As soon as your worry time is over, STOP.

Automatic Thinking

You are not just going to be focusing on those worries. You are also going to start looking at the automatic thoughts and situations from different perspectives. Cognitive behavioral therapy says that it is not the event that causes our emotional and behavioral reactions but the meaning we give to that event. This will help you develop more helpful ways of thinking.

Thought/situation/belief record sheet

What am I worried about? e.g., getting into medical school	What am I predicting? e.g., I will not get into medical school.	What emotion(s) am I feeling? (include the feeling and the intensity from 0-100%) e.g., sad (80%)
List my automatic thoughts. e.g., What if they don't accept me?	How much do I believe it will happen (0-100%)? 90%	

Exercise:

Evidence for	Evidence against
What is the worst that could happen?	What is the best that could happen?

What are the consequences of my worry about this?

Alternative / realistic thought. More balanced perspective.

Summary

- Worrying is a primary symptom of anxiety.
- Worrying often takes the form of "What if" questions.
- Anxiety and worrying are common.
- Anxiety, at normal levels, is helpful as it motivates us to act. When it is extreme, anxiety can cause debilitating symptoms for our mental health.
- There are different types of anxiety, such as fear and panic.
- Anxiety and worrying are maintained because of:
  - ✓ Beliefs
  - ✓ Attention to automatic thoughts
  - ✓ Useless strategies.
- It is important you keep practicing the exercises you learned through reading, as this will help you integrate them into your lifestyle.
- Expect setbacks and be patient. Change takes time!

CHAPTER 3

DEPRESSION

Overview and Research

This is one of the most common mental health disorders across the world. Depression has been linked to thoughtful and reflective thinking, particularly in individuals who have dysthymia, a longer-term, low-grade depression, often lasting for two or more years. You see this type of depression in high-achievement people, including lawyers. I want to be clear that depression is phasic/temporary and that it could be viewed as showing that you care about what upset you. That you care enough to respond with depression means something bothered you enough that you are taking time to think it through. You are sensitive and care about the well-being of others, and you're communicating that you need help at this time.

Depression affects our behavior, feelings, motivation, mood, and finally, our physical functioning and health. Lewinsohn's theory summarizes the symptoms of severe depression as follows:

- **Behavioral deficits**: isolation, social withdrawal, loss of appetite, slower speech, difficulty communicating, loss of sexual activity, loss of interest.

- **Behavioral excesses**: aggression, rebellion, feeling guilty, poor memory.

- **Emotional reactions**: sadness, irritability, loss of interest in relationships, nervousness, restlessness.

- **Lack of skills**: poor social skills, lack of humor, critical, indecisiveness.

- **Attitudes and motivation**: lack of self-confidence and motivation, low self-concept, self-blaming, self-critical, helplessness.

- **Physical symptoms**: sleep problems, hyperactivity, mood swings, low libido, loss of appetite, weight loss or gain, headaches, pain, constipation, dizziness, and other somatic complaints.

There are three critical types of depression: (1) major depression, (2) situational or reactional depression, and (3) bipolar disorder or manic depression.

Anxiety and depression are frequently and closely related, sharing the same features. American Psychologist Barlow David argues that anxiety and depression result from:

1. generic contributions,
2. early childhood experiences, like abuse or rejection, and
3. psychological vulnerabilities or personality tendencies that direct individuals toward a specific disorder.

Theories trying to explain depression describe, in short, that depression is the normal, natural reaction that we have when we lose something of value.

A survey at the Medical College of Virginia, for example, found that interpersonal losses (loss of a friend, marital problems, death) increased the risk of depression.

On the other hand, Seligman and Steinem suggest that baby boomers grew up to find a cold and unsupportive world. It is believed that our values and lifestyle affect our outlook on everything we do in our lives. The values determine what is good or bad, important and unimportant, and so on. Whenever our values are at risk, it is considered a loss. Thus, if we are depressed, it is crucial to realize the connection between values and losses, recognize the losses we may be responding to, and try to reduce these losses.

Biology is also vital in depression, as studies of identical twins and several generations within a family suggest that depression is partly inherited. Numbers of genes account for 41% to 46% of the variance in depression.

Another theory of the general adaptation syndrome suggests that exhaustion comes after an alarm reaction and resistance, making depressed people feel tired and drained of energy, with symptoms also regulated by the hypothalamus – a structure deep in your brain that maintains your body's internal balance.

Other theories suggest that various factors influence the transmission of nerve impulses, currently called neurotransmitters, in the brain, whereas too few neurotransmitters result in depression.

Believing just one of the abovementioned causes affects diagnosis and interferes with the individual taking responsibility for changing themselves. We cannot expect to magically treat depression with medication, primarily when the condition is caused by something else.

It is imperative to understand that symptoms found in the disorders mentioned above vary, as well as the judgment of the one who is making the diagnosis.

For example, a GP, clinical psychologist, partner, friend, or self-evaluation can all judge if someone is depressed. However, no one will agree, and that is causing complications in proper diagnosis and treatment. Thus, even when you know you are unhappy, you still get conflicting opinions from others, making it harder to get help.

WORKBOOK: TACKLE DEPRESSION
WITH CBT

Overview

Module 1: Overview of depression

Module 2: Thinking – Feeling connection

Module 3: ACT

Module 4: Self-compassion and mindfulness

Module 5: Narrative therapy – storytelling

Module 1: Overview of Depression

What is Depression?

Depression is a term used in plain English to express a variety of emotions, such as sorrow, frustration, disappointment, and, at times, apathy.

Many people who are suffering from depressive symptoms may begin to question whether there is something really wrong with them. One common concern is that they are becoming insane. Unfortunately, other people's emotions and statements, such as "Don't act like a child!" are not particularly helpful.

Although you may feel alone in your battle against these emotions, the fact is that many people experience these moods frequently, if not daily. In fact, it is expected that one out of every four people experience a seriously low mood at some point in their lives.

Depression may strike anyone at any age or stage of life. You may be an introvert or an extrovert, outgoing or reserved, young or old, male or female, rich or poor. You can get depressed regardless of your status. So, keep in mind that you are not alone in this.

In psychology, the term "depression" differs from the usual everyday feelings of symptoms in three main ways. Major depression is 1) more intense, 2) lasts two weeks or more, and 3) leads to an inability to function normally in day-to-day tasks.

As a disorder, depression is a set of experiences and behaviors that characterize depressed people. You may find yourself experiencing all or part of these feelings and behaviors. The number of symptoms and the level to which distinct symptoms are experienced vary greatly between individuals. We discuss these symptoms more below.

Mood

Depression is classified as a mood condition: People who are depressed experience a low mood that has lasted more than two weeks. Individuals suffering from moderate depression may not feel horrible all day but do experience a negative outlook and low mood. A great event may improve their mood, but even a slight disappointment might cause it to drop again. Low mood may remain throughout the day in severe depression, failing to rise even when pleasurable events occur. The mood may change during the day, being worse in the morning and somewhat better in the afternoon. This is known as 'diurnal variation,' and it is frequently associated with a more severe form of depression. In addition to low mood, the individual may experience feelings of inadequacy and worthlessness, guilt, anxiety, and anger.

Cognitive symptoms

People with depression tend to see life in negative lenses. Individuals who are depressed have low self-esteem and low self-confidence. They constantly think about how bad they feel, how hopeless everything is, and how bad life is.

Physical symptoms

People with depression may experience problems with sleep. Some have difficulty falling asleep. Others may wake up during the night or wake up early in the morning. Others may have difficulty staying awake.

The appetite changes and some people find themselves eating more than usual while others eat less. Body weight changes as well.

People with depression have lower sexual interest.

They also have less energy and less motivation and may stop doing things they used to enjoy.

Module 2: Thinking – Feeling Connection

The Thinking-Feeling Connection

People frequently assume that their moods and emotions are influenced by the behavior of others, external events, and the environment. "My partner made me so stressed," "My neighbor made me so upset," "The traffic lights made me feel so anxious," or "I'm feeling bad because I didn't get the job I wanted." We automatically assume that someone or something else is controlling our emotions.

We reach these conclusions without questioning whether or not the assumption is correct. However, if we learn how to stop analyzing, we will find that there is a process in between.

How Do Our Thoughts Affect Our Feelings?

What truly causes us to feel and behave in the manner we do is frequently not the circumstance or another person's words or actions but how we interpret that situation or that person's actions. How we perceive something or someone and what we think about it or them significantly impacts how we feel. Our emotions and actions are heavily influenced by our ideas and beliefs about an event.

Here's an example. Suppose you went to a job interview. As you talk to your future employer, you notice that he does not look directly at you but often at his mobile phone. How would you feel if you thought, "He is a very rude guy!" What if you thought, "I must be really failing in this? He seems not to like me."

At this time, you probably realized you felt different emotions as a result of these thoughts. In reality, we do not have much time to analyze our thoughts because they are automatic and happen instantly. But this is an example that our thoughts are there and affect the way we feel.

Often, we find it difficult to find words for our feelings. The words below can be a useful starting point for understanding the connection between our thoughts and feelings.

Words that describe feelings:

Angry, Triggered, Tired, Happy, Excited, Joyful, Annoyed, Unhappy, Anxious, Calm, Scared, Sad, Cheerful, Upset, Nervous, Irritated, Bored.

Automatic Thoughts

Just as we are not always conscious of the way we talk or walk, we are often unaware of our thoughts, varying from 70,000 to 100,000 thoughts every day.

Our thinking, even automatic, helps us interpret the world around us, explaining to us what is happening. It interprets events, sounds, smells, feelings and other stimuli. Thoughts come and go all the time, especially automatic thoughts, playing an important role in our well-being.

There are three kinds of automatic thoughts:

Neutral thoughts. For example: "I think I will go to the bank today."

Positive thoughts. For example: "I like dancing; I'm so good at it."

Negative thoughts. For example: "I cannot complete this task; I must be stupid."

How Do Our Thoughts Affect Our Feelings?

Automatic thoughts frequently represent fears and anxieties, but they may also be about anything we have ever seen, heard, or learned. Furthermore, it might be anything we know about from any source.

Negative automatic thoughts, on the other hand, are clearly the ones that could give us emotional pain. People who are depressed have bad views about themselves, the world around them, and their future. Modifying these negative beliefs may help you overcome your depression.

Cognitive behavioral therapy says that following an event, we give meaning to it through our thoughts, and then it starts to influence the way we feel.

These thoughts result in our physical and emotional reactions.

Event	Thoughts	Emotion	Behavior
Hit a bicyclist with the car	I will go to jail	Fear	Driving away with the car
My boss treats me unfairly	He must hate me	Anger, frustration	Defensive, disobedient

Automatic words…

- Can be thoughts, memories, sounds, or words that we automatically believe are valid.
- Can happen at any time, as they are automatic.
- Are ours, and they represent our experiences, values, culture, and knowledge.
- Are habitual, persistent and do not go away. They repeat over and over and the more resistant we are, the more persistent they get.

Feelings are not thoughts

When we initially try to distinguish between ideas and feelings, it is easy to get them mixed up. We may be accustomed to discussing thoughts and feelings as if they were two sides of the same coin. It is more beneficial to separate them and remember that feelings are not thoughts.

Try the following exercise and see if you can distinguish the feelings and thoughts in each scenario.

Exercise: Distinguish thoughts from feelings

Read the following scenarios and identify the feelings that may result from the thoughts.

Scenario A

You have had a tiring day at work, and you just arrived home to find dishes dirty in the sink, the faucet running, and your partner sitting in front of the television playing video games.

1) You think

"What a nightmare. I have had a long day and now I am coming home to this! Life is unfair! He doesn't care about me, only about himself!"

Possible feelings:

_____

_____

2) You think

"I must have done something to deserve this. I am a bad partner. I don't deserve him. He is right to ignore me."

Possible feelings:

_____

_____

Scenario B

One day, your boss asks you to go to the office for a meeting. As you arrive, you notice that the door is closed. You knock, and no one answers. You open the door and find your boss and all your colleagues standing there in front of you shouting "Surprise!" and singing "Happy Birthday."

1) You think

"Wow, what a nice surprise. I wasn't expecting this."

Possible feelings:

_____

_____

2) You think

"Everybody must like me."

The ABC Analysis

We've discussed how our thoughts influence how we feel. If we are joyful and thrilled, we have most likely been having positive thoughts and thinking about wonderful things. On the other hand, if we are nervous, depressed, or disturbed, we have most certainly been having negative thoughts (these are referred to as harmful thoughts because they lead to unpleasant feelings or unproductive behaviors). We all have moments when we consider things that make us sad or nervous; this is a natural part of life. However, if you frequently feel worried or nervous, you may need to evaluate your thoughts in order to enhance your mood.

Do these automatic thoughts lead to uncomfortable feelings? Then, the most effective thing to do is to change those unhelpful thoughts to helpful ones.

So, how do you go about doing that? To begin changing the way you feel, you must first learn to recognize when problematic automatic thoughts come and then try to replace them using the ABC analysis.

ABC Analysis

As mentioned above, there is an event that activates every behavior and thought. In the ABC analysis, we start to determine this Activating Event (A) by writing down the situation or the setting in which we had these uncomfortable feelings, such as depression. Write down the scene in detail, the way a camera would do. Just state the facts without explaining or describing any thoughts.

The following stage is to determine the 'C,' which stands for 'Consequences,' which comprises both your emotions and your behavior/action. Make a list of the words that best describe your emotions. Underline the word that best describes the feeling you were experiencing at that moment. Then, on a scale of 0 to 100, assess the intensity of this emotion. The greater the number, the stronger the reaction. Also make a note of any behavior or action you carried out. For example, closing all the doors and going to bed.

Now, remembering the circumstances and your emotions, find the 'B,' symbolizing your 'Beliefs' or thoughts, expectations, perceptions, and attitudes. For example: "What was I thinking about when the telephone started to ring?" and "What thoughts were going through my mind?"

Make a list of all your thoughts. When you've finished, study each thought and highlight the one most aligned with the predominant feeling you had during the 'A.' We'll refer to this as your hot thought, and on a scale of 0 to 100, rate how strongly you believe this.

Let's look at an example. Imagine walking into your boss's office feeling anxious. To do an ABC analysis, you might ask yourself, "How am I making myself anxious? What am I thinking?" You might identify a thought such as, "I don't want to be here." If you only had this thought, you'd probably not experience a strong emotion but only feel mildly anxious. If you do experience a strong emotional response to this thought, it probably indicates that there are other underlying thoughts. Therefore, "I don't want to be here" is only an initial thought, and you would need to discover what other unhelpful thoughts were present to invoke such a strong emotional response. For example, "Maybe he is going to fire me."

Exercise: ABC Record and thought diary

Your goal should be to become an expert at spotting your unhelpful thoughts.

A Activating Event	**B** Believable Thoughts	**C** Consequences	
What, where, when, external event or internal trigger (real or imagined)

For example: I got caught cheating in exams | What did I think at that time?

For example: I thought that they would terminate my studies | Consequences of believing the thought

For example: I started feeling anxious, and I was breathing fast. Therefore, I panicked and ran out of the exam room | Consequences of not believing the thought

For example: I understood what I did was wrong, so I apologized and I moved on |

Module 3: ACT

Acceptance and Commitment Therapy

Acceptance and Commitment Therapy (ACT) is a type of Cognitive Behavioral Therapy best described as a process in which people confront and modify their understanding of their past experiences. This means that when an individual has experienced something traumatic affecting them for the rest of their life, impacting their relationships and other aspects of their life, ACT will take over. It gives a new meaning to that event, helping the individual become more resilient and psychologically flexible. ACT helps the individual take control of their life.

Who will benefit?

ACT will be beneficial to individuals who have experienced traumatic events, tragedies, hurt, and loss and to those who want to gain control of their lives. ACT will give meaning to their experiences and allow them to change their pain into motivation for something greater and better.

How to use ACT

ACT is a process of self-expression and a helpful tool for finding what is important to you. It is also great because it helps you clarify your values and emphasizes action to increase well-being instead of keeping an apathetic stance because of your negative thoughts.

Worksheets

1. Values Bullseye

The values bullseye exercise helps you reflect and put your feelings into words while also helping you to understand what is important. It also establishes your values and how you want to live your life.

Step 1: Identifying Your values

The bullseye exercise begins similarly to other standard value-finding exercises. The first step is to identify your values and what is most important to you. What are your primary thoughts, feelings and actions that affect your life? After you identify your values, you will categorize them into four main categories: 1) leisure, 2) relationships, 3) personal growth and health, and 4) work and education.

1. Leisure refers to how you enjoy yourself, how you have fun or relax; recreation, your hobbies, activities for fun or rest. For example, adventure, connection with others, and experiences.

2. Relationships refer to intimacy, friendships, and connections with others. This category includes relationships with your parents, partners, children, relatives, friends, colleagues, and other social relationships. What kind of relationships do you want? How do you want to be in these relationships? For example, love, intimacy, respect, and connection with others.

3. Personal growth and health refer to your personal development, physical and mental health, spiritual development, and more. For example, health, physical appearance, and exercise.

4. Work and education refers to your education, career, knowledge, and development. What personal qualities do you want to possess? What skills do you want to develop? For example, accomplishment, aspiration, and justice.

You have probably noticed that some values fall into more than one category. This is perfectly normal. You will also see later that the same values may not show up in the same spot on the bullseye. Note that values are not goals and the easiest way to distinguish is to understand that goals are something you want to do, while values are how you want to live your life.

Step 2: Recognizing how close we are to living our values

After you've written down your values for each category, mark an X on the bullseye according to how closely you're living your values daily. The center of the bullseye indicates that this value guides your thoughts and activities every day. On the other hand, the outermost ring reveals that you aren't living by your ideals and that they aren't as important to you. Consider why you have placed your values in that particular ring. Can you think of any examples of this value demonstrated in your life? What would it look like to live following your values?

Take "connection with others" as an example. You may put this in the center of the bullseye and the leisure ring, but on the outside of the relationships ring. This suggests that when you have leisure time, you connect with others. But, in a relationship, you might not pay much attention to your connection with the other person. You can place an X on the bullseye for the values lacking attention and start to spend some time thinking about why you do so.

Work/Education   Leisure

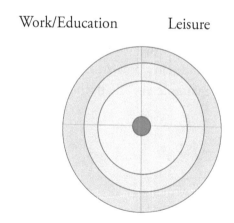

Personal Growth/Health   Relationships

Step 3: Identify obstacles that interfere with living our values

1) Now, based on what we have written in our areas of value, we need to write down the obstacles that interfere with living our lives as we want to. What stands between us and living our life as we would like? For example, for intimacy, the obstacle could include the fear of getting hurt emotionally or the fear of getting rejected. For building a more intimate relationship, obstacles could include working a lot of hours, neglecting our partner, and so on.

Obstacle 1: _____

Obstacle 2: _____

Obstacle 3: _____

2) Let's identify to what extent the obstacle prevents us from living our lives in the way we would like. On a scale of 1 to 7, where one means "doesn't prevent me at all," and seven means "prevents me completely," mark the number that best fits your estimate.

Obstacle	Doesn't prevent me at all (1)	2	3	4	5	6	Prevents me completely (7)
1							

2						
3						

Step 4: Create an action plan

With your bullseye in hand, it's time to draw up a strategy to live your values completely and to push those Xs closer to the center. Perhaps you need to develop healthier habits around something essential to you. Or maybe you could spend less time in toxic relationships. Identifying the obstacles that prevent you from living your values can provide you with an action plan. Is there anything more you should be doing? Or is it something you should do less?

Now, try to identify at least one action you are willing to take toward bringing each value closer to the center.

1. *Leisure.* For example, to have more fun, the action could be to work fewer hours and spend more time with myself or look for more adventures.

2. *Relationships.* For example, to build an intimate relationship, the action could be to focus on my well-being and my emotions, pay more attention to my partner, and be more expressive.

3. *Personal growth and health.* For example, I could take specialized courses or seek therapy if I want to improve my communication skills.

4. *Work and education.* For example, if I want a career, I could focus on improving my skills and knowledge in my field of work.

Module 4: Self-Compassion and Mindfulness

Compassion for oneself is fundamentally the same as compassion for others. Consider what it's like to feel compassion. To feel compassion for others, you must first recognize their pain. If you ignore the homeless person on the street, you won't be able to feel compassion for him and his experience. Having compassion means feeling the pain of others and suffering with them. When this happens, you experience a sense of warmth and care, and immediately, you want to help that person in any way. Compassion makes you realize that we are not perfect. We all can suffer and fail.

Self-compassion entails treating oneself the same way when you are having a tough time, failing, or noticing anything you don't like about yourself. Instead of just rejecting yourself, pause and ask, "This is extremely painful right now. How can I soothe myself in this moment?" Self-compassion implies you are compassionate and understanding when confronted with personal faults rather than relentlessly criticizing and blaming yourself for different deficiencies or weaknesses.

The three elements of self-compassion:

1. Self-kindness

Self-compassion means being warm and sympathetic toward ourselves when we struggle, fail, or feel inadequate rather than dismissing our sorrow or shaming ourselves. Self-compassionate individuals understand that being flawed, failing, and experiencing life issues is unavoidable. That's why they show kindness to themselves when presented with painful situations instead of being upset when life falls short of predetermined expectations.

2. Humanity

Frustration at not getting what we desire is frequently accompanied by an unreasonable sense of isolation - as if "I" am the only one who is suffering. However, all humans suffer. Self-compassion entails acknowledging that suffering and personal inadequacy are part of the common human experience – something that we all go through rather than something that only "I" goes through.

3. Mindfulness

Self-compassion also necessitates a balanced attitude to our unpleasant emotions so they are not suppressed or exaggerated. This results from linking our experiences to those of others who are also suffering. It also comes from being willing to notice our unpleasant thoughts and feelings with openness and clarity to retain them in conscious awareness. Mindfulness is a nonjudgmental state of mind in which one observes thoughts and feelings as they are without trying to conceal or reject them. Mindfulness helps you tune in to the present moment.

There are many ways to practice mindfulness. Some examples include:

Pay attention: Intentionally apply an accepting attention to everything you do. Find joy in simple pleasures. For example, smelling the roses.

Accept yourself: Try to treat yourself the way you would treat a friend. For example, I failed in physics but it is okay. I will succeed the next time.

Focus on your breathing: For example, when your thoughts are chaotic, sit down and take a deep breath. Close your eyes and focus on your breath as it moves in and out of your body.

Meditation: Meditation can be done in two ways: (1) sitting, (2) walking

1) Sit comfortably with your back straight, feet flat on the floor, and hands in your lap. Inhale through your nose, exhale from your mouth. Notice how your breath moves through your body. If your thoughts interrupt your meditation, return your attention to your breath.

2) Find a quiet place and begin to walk slowly. Focus on your walk, being aware of the physical sensations. When you reach the end of your path, turn and continue walking, paying attention to the sensations.

Mindfulness = Gratitude

Everyone can benefit from making an effort to practice mindfulness every day. Mindfulness can help you become more grateful and appreciative of the good things in your life. Therefore, start to notice and identify things you are grateful for. Be mindful of the small details in your daily life, and see how many good things you take for granted.

Expressing gratitude is more than being polite. It is about showing your true heartfelt feelings. For example, when we want to thank someone, we usually say "thank you." This time, take note of something good about them and genuinely appreciate it.

Exercise:

- Show your appreciation to someone who did something nice. For example, a stranger carried your groceries to the car. Say: "It was really kind of you to help me" or "Thank you for your kind deed."
- Express gratitude by paying it forward. For example, a stranger carried your groceries to the car, and you held the door open for a stranger behind you.
- Tell people how you feel and what they mean to you. For example, "Dad, thanks for raising me up the way you did," or "Mom, delicious dinner, thank you."

Module 5: Narrative Therapy/Storytelling

Narrative therapy/ Storytelling is a part of ACT that allows you to become aware of your strengths and values. It can also help you identify your skills, which can help you deal with problems in daily life.

How Narrative Therapy/Storytelling works

Writing about your problems can help you get insight into your strengths, values, emotions, and goals, which, in turn, can help you find effective solutions. After writing down your life story, you will be asked to complete a worksheet containing two exercises with questions. Answer the questions according to each exercise by providing as much detail as possible.

Life Story

The Past, Present, the Future

Writing a story about your life can help you bring attention to your experience and values. It will help you put your thoughts into words and use them to act on. You are expected to gain a greater sense of meaning, which can contribute to your happiness.

The Past

Write a story about your past and include any challenges you have experienced, how you overcame them, and what strengths or skills allowed you to do so.

The Present

Write a story about your present and describe your life. Who are you at this moment? How are you different from your past self? What challenges are you facing now? What are your strengths?

The Future

Write about your ideal future. How would you want your life to be ten years from now? How will you be different from the person you are now?

Worksheet – Answer the Questions:

Exercise 1

Write in detail about a traumatic event/situation that you faced recently.

How did you respond?

What is your biggest strength?

How could you use this strength to deal with the traumatic event?

Exercise 2

Write in detail about an event in which you felt rejected or disappointed.

How did you respond?

How did you cope with the event?

How would you handle it differently using your skills?

Summary

- The cause of depression is a combination of biological and psychological factors.
- Depression symptoms may include low mood, low energy, lack of motivation, a tendency to think negatively, guilt, anxiety, anger, and feelings of inadequacy and worthlessness.
- What drives us to feel the way we do is not other people or situations but rather our own thoughts and beliefs in response to them.
- There are three kinds of thoughts: neutral, positive, and negative.
- If we feel negative, it is because we are often thinking negatively.
- If we want to improve how we feel, we need to become aware of our thoughts and change them.
- Consistent and continuous practice of the strategies you learned will help you integrate them into your lifestyle.

CHAPTER 4

BIPOLAR DISORDER

WORKBOOK - USE CBT TO COMBAT BIPOLAR DISORDER

Overview

Module 1: Introduction to Bipolar Disorder

Module 2: Bipolar Disorder treatment options

Module 3: Relapse prevention self-monitoring

Module 4: Behavioral strategies for managing and preventing depression

Module 5: Cognitive strategies for depression management and prevention

Module 6: Preventing mania using cognitive strategies

Module 7: Preventing mania using behavioral strategies

Module 8: Self-management and coping with psychosocial stressors

Module 1: Introduction to Bipolar Disorder

Bipolar Illness, often known as Manic Depression, is a mood disorder. This indicates that people who suffer from this condition have strange or excessive mood changes. This condition causes patients to experience extreme emotional highs and lows, causing them to be both joyful and sad and making it difficult for them to be happy or satisfied. The medical term for this is bipolar disorder. The strong emotions are referred to as "manic episodes," while the negative moods are called "depressive episodes." These episodes can be moderate or severe and alter a person's thoughts, feelings, and behaviors. It's crucial to remember that various people may have different approaches to dealing with their disease, so it's vital to be aware of that. Some people, for example, experience only one bout of mania but many more instances of despair.

Bipolar Disorder affects around 1% of the population, which implies that one out of every 100 people may experience an episode that will likely need hospitalization. Both men and women are affected by this condition, which generally begins in their early to late twenties.

Maniac episodes

Mania is a really terrible mood that occurs as a result of this condition. It denotes an excessively happy, ecstatic, motivated, or furious state of mind. Hypomania is when your mood is somewhat elevated. Because the individual is still in touch with reality, it may often be treated without a hospital visit. However, it is quite simple to shift from hypomania to a manic episode, and this may happen very fast. Mania manifests itself in a variety of ways, including:

Irritability

The Oxford lexicon has a term for irritation that means "fast to become irritated or sensitive". Many people have a lot of ideas and thoughts when they are in a good mood. When it comes to thinking, individuals frequently find themselves well ahead of others. They've already developed a new concept before the people around them have fully grasped the previous one. They become enraged when others do not comprehend their ideas or passion for a new endeavor since they think swiftly.

Sleep is reduced

You feel more energized and don't need to sleep as much as you used to, which is one of the most prevalent indicators of mania and typically an early warning sign. People are usually kept awake and engaged in new ideas and initiatives by the quick flow of thoughts and ideas.

Thoughts that are insane

For people who are becoming insane, the rate at which they think increases. They go from one subject to the next at a rapid pace. Thoughts can sometimes travel so fast that they lose meaning, resulting in a jumbled, incomprehensible message that the person receiving it cannot comprehend.

Thoughts of grandeur

Many people suffering from mania believe they are more gifted than others or possess special powers. As the person's mood improves, they become more deluded. People frequently believe that they are renowned or in this world for a specific reason (often, religious beliefs can become intense and take on more significance than usual).

Poor decision-making

People's decision-making abilities may be harmed, and they may act in ways inconsistent with their beliefs or conventions.

Libido is excessive and uncontrolled

When a person is manic, the more libido they have, the more likely they are to make poor choices regarding who to have sex with.

Depressive episodes

Bipolar Disorder Diagnosis

A precise diagnosis will help you explore the many therapy choices available to manage your disease. An appropriate diagnosis is the first step in getting healthier this way. It's critical to remember that only your doctor, psychiatrist, or someone who has received mental health training can make an accurate diagnosis. Someone who's not a skilled mental health professional or doctor, isn't qualified.

The Diagnostic and Statistical Manual of Mental Disorders (DSM-IV), which includes definitions and criteria for these diseases, was used by the American Psychiatric Association in 1994 to classify people with bipolar illness.

The most prevalent of the bipolar mood disorders, Bipolar I Disorder, is also the most common. It is marked by full-blown manic episodes and extremely severe bouts of depression. People experience bad moods in a variety of ways, and each person may have a unique experience with the condition. Bipolar I illness, according to many experts, is a condition that reoccurs, with symptoms that come and go. It is critical to continue therapy even after the symptoms have subsided to avoid a repeat of the event.

People with Bipolar II Disorder have full-blown periods of sadness as well as episodes of hypomania (minimal manic symptoms) that nearly never progress to full-blown mania.

In Cyclothymic Disorder, short bursts of moderate melancholy and hypomania are prevalent. They're also mixed in with bursts of normal mood. Even if a person with cyclothymic illness does not experience significant depression or mania, they might develop bipolar I or II disorder.

Bipolar I and II patients may experience a lot of mood fluctuations. In a given year, more than four bouts of sadness, hypomania, and/or psychosis can occur in one person. Rapid Cycling is a term used to describe these folks. They have a tendency to alternate between severe emotional states and brief moments of well-being.

Bipolar disorder can be caused by a number of factors, Although not by an event, or experience. It also isn't caused by a person but may be the result of a variety of factors that interact. Because of these factors, some people develop this condition. In this section, we'll show you how all of these elements come together to cause bipolar disorder. A stress vulnerability model. is the term for this model.

When we examine this paradigm, we begin by considering three key factors: genetic vulnerability, physiologic vulnerability, and socioenvironmental stress (or life stress).

Genetics

Bipolar disorder has a high chance of being handed on from generation to generation. People who have first-degree relatives with the illness are more prone to have the illness themselves. Children of bipolar parents have an 8% probability of developing the disorder, compared to 1% in the general population. Children with bipolar parents are more prone to develop Unipolar Depression (12%), (sadness without mania). Identical twins are more likely than fraternal twins to suffer from bipolar disorder because they are more likely to share the same genetics. These findings imply that, to some extent, this illness is passed down in families. They also suggest that there might be other reasons influencing its development.

Vulnerability to biological threats

This refers to biochemical abnormalities in the brain, which might make a person more prone to mood swings. If brain chemicals are imbalanced or not acting correctly, "high" and "low" emotions might occur.

Stress is caused by social and environmental factors

When stressful events or situations occur in a person's life, such as getting married, having children, moving to a new home, or experiencing a loss, they might feel agitated, frustrated, or nervous. The interaction of these three factors helps explain why someone has bipolar disorder. Even if a person is genetically or physiologically susceptible, they may not develop bipolar illness. How people deal with stress in their lives impacts on their vulnerabilities. A person with a family history of diabetes, for example, may avoid developing diabetes if they watch what they eat and exercise regularly. As a result, we'll discuss elements that can be both protective and hazardous.

Protective factors and those that are risky

Several factors increase the chances of someone who is currently unwell being sick again. Risk factors include those who abuse alcohol or drugs, have poor coping skills, don't stick to a routine, have conflicts with their friends, or experience stressful occurrences. Protective factors are things that can help a person stay healthy while they are in danger of becoming unwell. These things can also assist a vulnerable individual in maintaining their health. Protective variables include solid coping skills, strong social support networks, effective communication and problem-solving abilities, and more. This is because people are likely to develop the condition if they have more risk factors than protective factors. This approach also applies when considering the possibility of a repetition.

The progression of the condition

Even though some people with bipolar illness may experience extended periods of normal emotions, the majority of persons with the diagnosis will experience many manic and depressed episodes throughout their lives. The number of manic and depressive episodes, as well as the frequency with which they occur, will vary from person to person. Some people only have two or three episodes in their lives, while others get four or more in a year, known as a "rapid cycle." Patients with bipolar disorder must learn how to control their disease and prevent having future episodes, regardless of the pattern.

Bipolar Disorder has several characteristics.

The following are the most prevalent symptoms of bipolar disorder: Anxiety and despair persist in your mood.

Depressed people frequently state that they are always unhappy and hopeless. They might not want to eat or enjoy the things they formerly did.

Sleep deprivation or interruption

Sad people frequently have difficulties sleeping, which might be due to their increased stress levels. They wake up often during the night and can't return to sleep because they are unable to fall asleep. They may also be concerned about events that may occur the following day, or they may wake up early in the morning and be unable to get back to sleep.

Feelings of worthlessness or hopelessness

People frequently believe they are useless and worthless because they are burdened with the feeling that they can't assist anyone. People may consider how bleak the situation is and how horrible things may get in the future.

A lack of sexual desire

When a person is sad, they lose interest in social activities and sex.

Concentration difficulties

The person's thinking may slow down, causing difficulty in making judgments. It can be difficult for them to concentrate when they try to read a book or go shopping. Because of this, a person may get agitated or uneasy.

Suicidal ideation

When a person's sentiments of hopelessness and despair become overwhelming, they may consider suicide or make preparations to kill themselves.

Episodes with a variety of themes

A mixed episode occurs when you experience both depression and manic symptoms practically every day for a lengthy period. There are mood swings, such as anger, euphoria, and sorrow, as well as sleeplessness, agitation, hallucinations and delusions, suicidal thoughts, and more.

Keeping Track of Your Symptoms

What type of symptoms are you experiencing? On the following page, there is a sheet labeled "Symptom Record."

If you're having a good day, write down how you're feeling. When you are not sad, hypomanic, or manic, you are in this state. Consider how you feel, what you think, and what you do or don't do, whether you're sad, hypomanic, or manic in this scenario. Then, jot down these symptoms as well.

Finally, you'll be able to spot any early warning indications that your body sends out when anything is awry.

Symptom Record

There are a number of questions on this worksheet that you might want to ask yourself.

- What should I do if I don't have any symptoms?

- How do things alter in my life when I'm sad or maniacal?

- Do my feelings about myself, other people, and the future alter when I'm sad, manic, or feeling better?

- When I'm flashing signs, what do other people observe about me?

- What type of feedback do I get from others?

Practice the Stress-Vulnerability Worksheet. Learn how to lower risk variables and increase protection so you can better manage your disease and reduce your risk of relapsing.

Worksheet on Stress and Vulnerability

Factors of Vulnerability: What variables do you believe enhanced your risk of having bipolar disorder or experiencing a depressed, hypomanic, or manic episode?

Risk Factors: What factors could make you more likely to have a depressed, hypomanic, or manic episode?

Protective Factors: What are some of your resources and strengths that might reduce your chances of having a depressed, hypomanic, or manic episode?

Checklist for Stress: Did anything in your life cause you stress before you experienced a depressive, hypomanic, or manic episode?

Module 2: Bipolar Disorder Treatment Options

Introduction

Medication is the conventional therapy for bipolar illness to control or eliminate symptoms and subsequently maintain symptom-free status by preventing relapse. Working together with your doctor is the best approach to utilizing medicine. Some people may respond well to one type of treatment and experience few side effects, while others may benefit from another. As a result, it's critical to monitor your medication's effects and speak with your doctor if you have any concerns.

The fundamentals of medication administration

1. You must follow the guidelines and pay attention to your symptoms and side effects in order to receive the greatest outcomes from taking medication.

2. If you have any adverse effects, notify your doctor as soon as possible to minimize long-term suffering. You mustn't stop taking your medication without first consulting your doctor. A manic or depressed episode may recur. It may happen again as a result of this.

3: You should avoid alcohol, illicit substances, and other prescribed medications since they can make your bipolar disorder medication less effective and produce more negative effects. You should inform your doctor about all other drugs and substances you're taking so that none of them interfere with your bipolar disorder prescription. Substance misuse has been found in studies to harm the course and outcome of bipolar illness. It might possibly play a role in relapse and recurrent episodes.

4. The best method to manage bipolar disorder is to monitor your symptoms and side effects, then work with your doctor to adjust your medication dosages or types.

Stages of treatment

There are generally three rounds of medical treatment for persons with bipolar illness: Acute care, continuation care, and maintenance care. The most crucial thing to do if you're experiencing mania, hypomania, or significant depression is to reduce or eliminate the symptoms so you can return to your usual level of everyday functioning. It might last anywhere from 6 weeks to 6 months throughout this short-term therapeutic period. Finding the finest treatments with the fewest side effects might take a long time.

You'll need to continue therapy for another 4 to 9 months after you begin it. The key aim during this phase is to maintain the symptom-free condition by ensuring that the most recent mood episode does not recur.

The maintenance phase, the third phase, is critical for anyone suffering from bipolar illness. The purpose of maintenance treatment is to prevent mania, hypomania, or depression from reoccurring or to reduce the frequency of recurrence. Maintenance treatment for persons with bipolar illness, like diabetes or high blood pressure, might extend for five years, ten years, or perhaps the remainder of their life. The more time you have to accomplish the things in life essential to you, the longer you will be symptom-free.

When a patient receiving therapy is prescribed medication, they must take it daily. Only use paracetamol and antibiotics if you have a headache or an infection. People with bipolar illness must take their meds at the same dose every day, even on good and bad days.

Bipolar Disorder Medication: This disease is treated with a variety of medications.

Mood elevator

A mood stabilizer is a medicine used to reduce the likelihood of having another bout of mania or depression, thus the name. They assist patients with bipolar illness in the initial stages of recovery. Depending on their symptoms, antipsychotics or antidepressants may be prescribed to people with this illness. A mood stabilizer is a long-term medication that helps to keep a person's mood calm but does not address the initial problem. This isn't to say you shouldn't use mood stabilizers. The medication will keep you steady. Lithium carbonate, sodium valproate, and lamotrigine are commonly used by those who need to keep their emotions in check. These medications can be used alone or in combination with other treatments.

Antidepressants

Antidepressants can sometimes be used with mood stabilizers as part of a medical treatment plan. For people with bipolar illness, no one antidepressant performs better than the others. Because antidepressants can cause a person to move from normal to manic or hypomanic behavior, there is a strong possibility that they will do so. Because all antidepressants appear to operate the same and take a long time to work, side effects are frequently the deciding factor in which antidepressants are prescribed. If you don't like one type of antidepressant, you might be able to switch to another or even one from the same class.

- SSRIs, (selective serotonin reuptake inhibitors): fluoxetine, paroxetine, and sertraline are examples.
- SNRIs, (serotonin and norepinephrine reuptake inhibitors) such as venlafaxine, duloxetine, and amitriptyline, which block serotonin and noradrenaline reuptake.
- Amitriptyline, desipramine, dothiepin, and lorazepam are examples of tricyclics. They aren't as commonly prescribed as other antidepressants.
- Monoamine oxidase inhibitors (MAOIs) such as phenelzine.

Antidepressants can have a variety of adverse effects depending on the medicine. Some older people may find them more annoying. Most of the time, adverse effects appear soon or when the dose is increased. Lower dosages produce fewer negative effects in most cases, and newer drugs have fewer side effects in the short and long term.

It's critical to understand the distinction between depressive symptoms and medication side effects. Discuss this with your doctor before beginning to take the medication. Some drugs might have side effects that are strikingly similar to depressive symptoms, such as insomnia and sex issues.

Antipsychotic medications

Antipsychotics are used to aid people in the early stages of the condition. They can also help people with the illness over a long period. These can be used with mood stabilizers to help individuals sleep, regulate psychotic symptoms, including hallucinations and delusions, and be less irritable and impulsive. They are also used as mood stabilizers in continuation and maintenance therapy to help patients avoid having psychotic or manic symptoms reappear.

Antipsychotics are divided into two categories: first-generation and second-generation antipsychotics. Olanzapine and quetiapine are two of the most prescribed second-generation antipsychotics (such as chlorpromazine and haloperidol).

Weight gain, tiredness, dizziness, stomachache, dry mouth, and constipation are some of the adverse effects of second-generation antipsychotic medications. Minimize these negative effects by using the lowest dosage of drugs required. While you're taking these medications, it's also a good idea for your doctor to monitor your weight, blood pressure, blood sugar, and cholesterol.

Benzodiazepines

There are also benzodiazepines, which are a class of medications that can aid persons with bipolar illness (e.g., clonazepam, diazepam). These drugs are sometimes used with other drugs, such as mood stabilizers and antipsychotics, to aid sleep, reduce psychomotor agitation, and slow racing thoughts. Because long-term use of benzodiazepines can develop tolerance and dependency, they are normally only taken for a brief period. Drowsiness, dizziness, a "hungover" sensation, and inability to keep stable are only a few of the benzodiazepine adverse effects.

Other things to consider: Various people respond to these drugs differently. A medicine that works well for one individual may not work for another or may be difficult to take. Many factors impact how drugs function, including gender, age, heredity, metabolism, and so on. Each individual must be prescribed medication that is appropriate for them. It is critical to consider the following factors.

- You must tell your doctor about any additional health concerns you have so they can determine the appropriate drugs for you. Medical issues can influence the medications you are allowed to take and the dose.
- Let your doctor know if you're taking other medications (including over-the-counter and natural therapies). There may be interactions between these therapies and the medications you're taking if you have bipolar disorder. If you're intending to get pregnant, talk to your doctor about which medications you can use.

Keeping track of your medications

You must talk to your prescribing doctor or psychiatrist about anything and everything. Most people who don't enjoy or respond well to one type of drug may benefit from trying a different one. Use this spreadsheet to keep track of the medications you're taking, how much you're taking, and any potential adverse effects. Keep track of how you feel after taking the drug to see if it is effective. If you are concerned about how you are feeling, make sure you notify your doctor about your pharmaceutical therapy. This might also serve as a record of the medications you've taken previously.

Use the area at the bottom of the page to jot down some questions you'd want to ask your doctor regarding your medicine or condition.

	Name and Type of Medication	Dosage	Notes
Current			

Past			

Questions I might have for my doctor

Psychosocial Therapy

Even though effective treatments for bipolar illness have been discovered, many patients still have episodes and relapses. Even if the symptoms between episodes aren't severe enough to be classified as a full-fledged episode, they might cause pain and make it difficult to do activities like go to school or work. It could be that you don't take your medications, drink alcohol or drugs, are under a lot of stress, or have a lot of between-episode symptoms. To enhance their patients' health and quality of life, mental health practitioners have tried psychotherapy and psychosocial therapies, as well as taking their patients' medications.

Psychosocial therapies for bipolar illness assist patients in learning more about their disease, discovering early warning signs and triggers for episodes, and helping them develop action plans to avoid having another episode.

CBT stands for Cognitive Behavioral Therapy.

Many sorts of adult mental health disorders have been well-studied, and Cognitive Behavioral Therapy (CBT) is one of the most effective treatments. Many additional mental diseases, such as unipolar depression, anxiety disorders, and eating disorders, have been treated using CBT. It is now used to treat bipolar disorder.

CBT is a controlled, time-limited treatment that should only be utilized for a short period. Collaboration between the therapist and the patient and the patient's active participation in the treatment's goals are two of the most significant aspects of this style of therapy.

CBT also focuses on problem-solving techniques. The basic purpose of CBT is to teach patients how their ideas and beliefs influence how they respond to circumstances and with people. Patients are also taught how to employ tools from the CBT technique to improve their response.

CBT can be used to educate bipolar patients about their illness and assist them in adjusting to their new lives. CBT can also help patients manage everyday pressures by teaching them how to monitor and control their thoughts, feelings, and actions, as well as preparing them to deal with symptoms in between episodes.

Module 3: Relapse Prevention Through Self-Monitoring

Self-Monitoring

A storm is on its way. What evidence do we have? The sky may be gloomy and ominous, with rain clouds forming, and the wind will speed up. We could stay at home even if we don't want to be affected by the storm's harshest consequences. We'd probably shut all the windows and doors, bring our clothes in from the line, and secure any loose items outside the home. Bipolar patients can also make efforts to avoid a full-blown episode of depression and mania if they become more aware of the early symptoms that a mood episode is about to begin.

If you have bipolar disorder, you may be on the verge of a manic or depressive episode. If you see it coming, you can intervene promptly to prevent a mood swing. To be able to forecast when an episode is about to begin, bipolar patients must learn to understand their own early warning signs and symptoms of their condition. Each person's indicators and symptoms are unique, although many will be the same for others.

You should keep an eye on early indicators and symptoms of a mood episode if you can recognize them. It won't help if you're aware of your early warning signs and symptoms but don't pay attention to when they first appear. Also, even if a person understands that dark and ominous clouds indicate rain, thunder, and lightning and move swiftly, they may still be caught in a storm if they are too preoccupied with their book to glance around. As a result, self-monitoring is critical in order to intervene early and prevent relapse.

Keeping track of one's emotions

Keeping track of your mood during the day is the first step in self-monitoring. Consider how you felt today. Was my mood in the middle of the spectrum, or was it a touch low or high? Is this really that low? What do you mean by that? Rate your mood on a scale of -5 (depressed) to +5 (happy) (manic). Keep a daily journal of how you're feeling.

Keep note of your moods and how they vary using the worksheet on the following page. Try it for a week to see if you can see any patterns in your mood swings. Make a list of joyful and sad experiences in your life. Bring your completed mood-tracking worksheets to your doctor or mental health practitioner to discuss your findings.

Keep an eye on your signs and symptoms

Another method to keep an eye on yourself is to be aware of any indications and symptoms that might indicate that you're having a depressed, manic, or mixed episode. Many of these symptoms may begin to worry you after a few days, so you may want to take action. We'll talk about planned early interventions a little bit later.

Use the worksheet provided to record any symptoms that have made it difficult for you to do the majority of your everyday responsibilities.

Keeping track of one's emotions

Fill in the graph below throughout the next week to monitor how your mood varies each day.

Over the next week, keep track of how your mood changes on a daily basis by sensing the following.

Mania	Mon	Tues	Wed
4			
3			
2			
1			
0			
-1			
-2			
-3			
-4			
Depression			

Mania	Thurs	Fri	Sat	Sun
4				
3				
2				
1				
0				
-1				
-2				
-3				
-4				
Depression				

Symptom Tracking Sheet

If you have had any of the symptoms in the following table, tick on the record sheet below each day. If they have affected most of your daily activities, you need to write them down. Some of these symptoms may have happened in a certain way, and you might want to write down any of your thoughts about that.

Mania	Mon	Tues	Wed
Depressed mood			

Lack of interest/ pleasure			
Change in appetite			
Inability to sleep/sleeping too much			
Fatigue/ loss of energy			
Elevated or irritable mood			
Racing thoughts			
Problems with concentration			
Thoughts of suicide			
Anger			

Mania	Thurs	Fri	Sat	Sun
Depressed mood				
Lack of interest/ pleasure				
Change in appetite				

Inability to sleep/sleeping too much				
Fatigue/loss of energy				
Elevated or irritable mood				
Racing thoughts				
Problems with concentration				
Thoughts of suicide				
Anger				

In which situations/activities do I feel these behaviors?

_____

_____

Detecting Early Warning Signs and Keeping an Eye on Them

When you start to experience a relapse or an episode returns, it's critical to know what to watch for. Many people with bipolar illness believe they can't foresee when they'll have an episode. Nevertheless, researchers have discovered that many can recall the early warning symptoms that appear before a full-blown episode. Bipolar individuals have stated that they were more active and didn't require as much sleep. They also reported that their mood had improved. And they did not need as much sleep as they had previously. Although there were significant variances in the early warning signals experienced by patients, these symptoms seemed to be the same for each patient in subsequent episodes. Even while some early warning signals may be unique to each patient, they appear to be quite effective at forecasting the onset of a mood episode for each individual.

If you think back far enough, you might recall the Symptom Record from Module 1. If you had completed the worksheet, you would have identified and noted your normal symptoms of mania and depression. You would have been able to distinguish them from how you are when you are not experiencing an episode. You'll need to do a more thorough examination to discover your early indicators of mania and sadness. Ask yourself, "What am I like when my mood is modestly high and considerably elevated?" What do I look like and do during mild and moderate depression? Make a note of each one on the Early Warning Signs Worksheet on the next page. Consider the three or four most prevalent early indicators of mania and depression once you've written them down. Will you be able to distinguish between these symptoms if they occur again? It's a good idea to talk to your doctor or other health care practitioner about this worksheet.

Early Intervention Preparation

The next stage is to make a plan for what you'll do if you start to show signs of a big depressive or manic episode. Use the worksheet on page 7 of the book to keep track of your early intervention plans. When the moment comes, it's critical to be prepared and know what to do. Plan what you'll say, what you'll do, and what you'll ask your friends and family to do, among other things. For instance, if you realize that your activity level has increased and you're becoming restless, you should see your doctor. After you want to buy shoes, you may ask a buddy to keep your credit card or invite a relative over when you stop phoning them. You might also ask your friends and family to say particular things to you to indicate that you are unwell. It's a good idea to let them know the easiest method to avoid bothering you. Writing down your early intervention plans and keeping them in a convenient location is the best method to keep track of them. You might, for example, keep them on your desk or the refrigerator.

My plan of action for relapse prevention:

What I would do to prevent a full-blown mania episode	What would I do to prevent a full-blown depressive episode

What I would ask my friends or family to do for me	What I would ask my friends or family to do for me
What I would ask my friends or family to say to me	What I would ask my friends or family to say to me

Module 4: Behavioral Tips for Managing and Preventing Depression:

The Cycle of Depression

When someone has depression, their life, daily routines, and behavior can change in a big way. Often, these changes can make the depression worse and keep the person who is depressed from getting better.

Some people who are depressed don't have the energy or motivation to do things, so they don't do their daily tasks and responsibilities, or they let other people make the decisions. You may have seen these changes in yourself when you are depressed.

When you become less active, you may become even less motivated and more lazy. When you stop doing the things you used to enjoy, you don't get to feel good and have good memories. Your depression could get worse, and this could turn into a never-ending cycle.

The same thing can happen if someone starts skipping a few tasks and responsibilities at work or home. The list may start to grow. So, when a depressed person thinks about all the things they have to do, they might feel overwhelmed by how many things they haven't done. This may make them feel bad or think they aren't very good or even a failure. This will also keep the cycle of depression going on.

The Depression Cycle

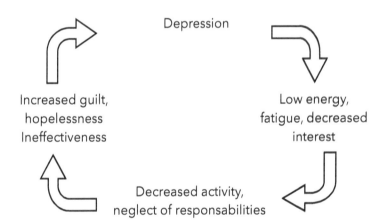

Depression

Increased guilt,
hopelessness
Ineffectiveness

Low energy,
fatigue, decreased
interest

Decreased activity,
neglect of responsabilities

Reversing the Cycle of Depression

The first thing you can do to break the cycle of depression is to get more active, especially in things that make you happy, and finish your list of tasks and responsibilities. However, it's important to remember to do this in a way that is both realistic and achievable so that you set yourself up for success. People who become more active have a lot of good things to say about it.

You will feel better if you do something. At the very least, when you start to do something, your mind has something else to think about. Even small steps can help you feel like you're moving forward and taking back control of your life. This can make you feel like you've achieved something. You might even enjoy and be happy with the things you do.

People who do a lot of things feel less tired. Most of the time, when you are physically tired, you need to rest. However, when you're down, the opposite is true. There is no good reason to sleep more and do nothing. If you don't do any work, your mind can think about things that make you sad, and you will feel even worse.

You can think more clearly if you do something. As soon as you start, you might see some problems in your life in a new light. It also may help to clear your thoughts. Your mind shifts its attention because of the activity.

It's called a "behavioral strategy," and involves planning activities for your week, like tackling small tasks and doing things that make you happy.

Do some pleasant or fun things and some simple things for yourself this coming week with the worksheet that comes next. Think of it as an experiment and see if you feel better after you do some things you enjoy. Do some chores or run errands, but don't forget to have some fun, too, when you plan your trip.

It will look like this if you keep to your plan and get more active.

Reversing the Depression Cycle

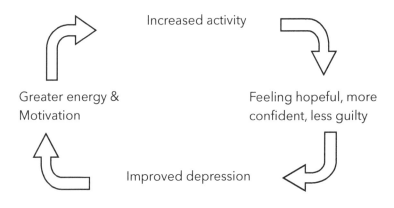

This behavioral strategy not only lifts your depression but stops it from coming back again, which is good for you. Remember to keep a good balance in your life between work and fun.

Worksheet on Behavioral Activation

This game is both fun and rewarding.

One way to fight depression is to plan some fun for yourself. It's easy to improve your mood and energy level by doing simple things you find fun. However, because you're depressed right now, you might not enjoy an activity as much as you did when you were not depressed. But don't just do one or two things. Keep going, and you'll start to feel better. Try it out and see!

You may also want to do some simple tasks or responsibilities that you haven't done in a while. Often, when you finish a task, you will be more motivated and have a sense of pride. Start with simple and doable tasks. Remember, though, that it's important to have both responsibilities and fun things in your life. Try not to spend too much time on one thing and not enough on the other.

Before and after the activity, use the following scale to rate how depressed you were, how happy you were, and how good you felt.

0	1	2	3	4	5
None	Slight	Mild	Moderate	Very high	Extreme

Note the activity and date, your state of depression and/or pleasure, and your achievement.

Before

_____

_____

After

_____

_____

Pleasurable activities catalog

The following is a list of activities that might be pleasurable for you. Feel free to add your own activities to the list.

1. Going to a party

2. Listening to music

3. Researching a topic of interest

4. Jogging

5. Spending time in nature

6. Learning a new language

7. Working

8. Going on a city tour

9. Going to the beach

10. Going ice skating

11. Enjoying ice cream

12. Washing my car

13. Playing soccer

14. Buying clothes

15. Going to the gym

16. Saying I love you

17. Listening to an audiobook

18. Baking

19. Doing arts and crafts

20. Flying kites

21. Listening to classical music

22. Travelling

23. Origami

24. Lighting candles

25. *Flirting*

26. *Going to the ballet*

27. *Buying gifts*

28. *Scuba diving*

29. *Daydreaming*

30. *Watching animals*

Weekly activity schedule

Record your activities for the coming week. Make sure you add fun and pleasurable activities as well as daily responsibilities and duties. Keep a balance.

Mon	Tues	Weds	Thurs	Fri	Sat	Sun
Before 13:00 pm						
After 13:01 pm						

Module 5: Cognitive Strategies for Depression Management and Prevention

Feelings and ideas

People frequently believe that events beyond their control and the actions of others impact their moods and emotions. "My employer made me frightened," "My spouse made me upset," "This trip to the south made me feel so calm," or "I'm depressed since I didn't get the job," are just a few instances. What is the assumption that these assertions are based on? Someone or something else had a significant effect on how we felt. Before making these judgments, we don't consider if this assumption is correct. However, if we consider how an external event impacts our emotions, we will discover that there is a middle ground.

How Our Thoughts Affect Our Emotions

Most of the time, it's not the scenario or the words and actions of another person that make us feel and act the way we do, but how we think about that situation or that person. Several factors influence how we feel. What we think and believe about an incident has a significant influence on our emotions and behaviors. We don't often think about how we walk or drive while we're out and about. We don't always think about how we think. Some of our thought processes are so habitual that we don't even notice them. When we drive, the same thing happens: when things are automated, we may not even notice them. On the other hand, our automatic thoughts have a significant impact on how we feel.

Here's one to use as an example: If you go to a party, your host may tell you that Mike is also there. You notice that he doesn't always look at you while you're talking to him; instead, he looks around the room. If you're thinking, "Oh, he's so obnoxious! I'm at a loss for words! He won't even look at me when I'm speaking to him. Mike must think I'm ugly and uninteresting. I must be a boring person. People don't want to talk to me." What if you thought to yourself, "Mike must be waiting for a buddy to arrive. Perhaps he's feeling a little tense." You may have observed that these separate thoughts caused you to experience different feelings. Our ideas and beliefs are so natural and happen so swiftly that we frequently don't even realize we have them. They are there, nonetheless, and make us feel different.

Thoughts are not the same as feelings, and they are not the same thing.

It's easy to get our ideas and feelings mixed up when we start separating them. We frequently discuss our ideas and feelings as if they were one and the same. It's best to keep them distinct and remember that feelings are not the same as ideas. Many times, you'll hear someone remark, "I believe I'm anxious," but what they're really thinking is, "Everyone is going to laugh at me."

or "I get the impression my boyfriend doesn't value the present I bought him." or "I don't believe my spouse appreciates the gift I got for him, and it hurts me."

To see if you can figure out the probable sentiments and ideas in each of the stories, try the next task. When writing, remember that you should aim to separate your thoughts from your feelings.

The process of putting things together

Those who desire to accomplish something.

The First Part: Examine the following situations and consider how the self-statements could make you feel.

The first scenario involves a hard and exhausting day at work. You assisted a buddy in moving boxes of stationery and office equipment. Your cream-colored carpet has two muddy footprints from your kid and his dog. They make their way from the front door to the back door.

"What? N@!#*M!! This is what I come home to after a long day at work. Is this something I deserved? It was cleaned only a few weeks ago. That disobedient kid! He is entirely concerned about himself. That greedy, thoughtless boy is so irritating. For the next two years, I'm going to keep him away from me!"

There are a variety of scenarios that might occur:

"I've told him a thousand times not to bring the dog inside the house, but he ignores me. Even the most basic rules are disobeyed by my children. I must be a lousy mother. I must be a nasty person. I can't seem to do anything right."

Another scenario might be:

Your folks invite you home for supper one evening. As soon as you arrive, you see there are no lights. You ring the doorbell, but no one answers. When you turn the doorknob, you notice it's not locked. When you walk into the house, there's no light. "Surprise!" you hear a chorus of people exclaim. When the lights turn on, they sing "Happy Birthday" to you.

You tell yourself, "Oh my goodness! This is fantastic." It was my birthday, and I had completely forgotten about it! What a wonderful surprise! James and Bertha were also there. They live on the outskirts of town. Because they threw me this party, everyone must think I'm special.

Fill in the blanks with the self-statements that made you feel the way you did in the scenarios below.

a. When you return home, you find a note from your flatmate informing you that they have moved out. They've taken all they have. Their portion of the rent is also unpaid.

A) You tell yourself, "This irritates me."

B) You tell yourself: When you are injured, you experience the following emotions.

b. After you've finished cooking for yourself and your companion, the following will occur: Your spouse called to say they'd have to work late and wouldn't be able to cook supper.

A) You tell yourself, "I'm not happy with how things turned out."

B) You tell yourself, "I'm worried about my feelings."

If you do this, you will feel better.

We've discussed how our ideas may affect how we feel. It's likely that if we're happy and thrilled, we've been thinking positive thoughts and thinking about positive things that make us happy. If we are nervous, depressed, or unhappy, on the other hand, we have probably been thinking negative ideas, which are causing us to feel that way. These ideas are labeled as unhelpful because they make us feel awful or drive us to do actions that are harmful to our health. We will inevitably think about things that make us unhappy or angry at some time in our lives. Depressed people may need to examine their thinking patterns in order to feel better.

What are the kinds of ideas that aren't good? Unhelpful ideas in this situation are pessimistic, exaggerating the possibilities of something unpleasant happening, or imposing unrealistic expectations on yourself and others. These are also known as "unhelpful thinking styles" since they are habitual patterns of thinking that make individuals feel terrible.

What options do I have now?

Plenty! There are several things you may do to improve your mood. The following recommendation has proven to be rather useful. Many people believe the best thing they can do is to replace the negative ideas that make them feel miserable with more positive ones. Yeah? How are you going to do that? A Thought Diary is included on the next page to help you organize and modify your own ideas.

To begin, write down a negative incident or condition, such as depression. Then, try to recall how or what you felt. Ask yourself, "What am I thinking about right now?"

What are the signs that I'm having a poor day? It's important to remember that negative ideas make you feel lousy.

The next stage is to think creatively. You may accomplish this by considering alternative explanations and seeing a subject from many angles. "What other perspectives may I take on this situation?" you might wonder. What could someone else's perspective be on this? It's unclear what else may be causing this.

What should be your last action? Then, come up with a new perspective on it. This is your fresh, well-balanced, and practical thinking. Balanced and practical thoughts or viewpoints consider multiple points of view and make you feel better. Substitute this fresh, balanced, and useful thinking for your old, unhelpful one. It should enhance your attitude and make you feel better.

It demonstrates how you may keep track of your ideas in a thought journal like the one below. Each column has prompts to help you move through the procedure quickly and simply. Be straightforward and clear in your writing. When you're finished, work through this process with a tale from your own life in the thought notebook on the following page.

My Thought Diary

What happened?	What was I thinking?	How can I think differently?
e.g., When my partner came home, he said hi but didn't kiss me like he usually does	He must be tired of me. He doesn't care about me.	He might have had a difficult day at work. He might be tired.

Module 6: Preventing Mania with Cognitive Strategies

People with bipolar illness typically regard the onset of mania or hypomania as a positive sign. Individuals frequently feel enthusiastic, eager, and hopeful when they're in a good mood. However, other people report that irritability and agitation, as well as dysphoria and pleasure, are typical at the start of mania or hypomania. Both may occur at the beginning of a mania or hypomania episode. People experiencing mixed episodes might go from a pleasant mood to extreme anger in a matter of minutes.

Symptoms of mania, hypomania, or mixed episodes usually appear over a few days or weeks. People frequently observe a pattern in the changes in their symptoms over time. Hypomania or mania, for example, may begin with one symptom, such as sleeplessness, and then progress to additional symptoms (e.g., increased sexual interest and feelings of euphoria). People's minds can also shift or become more interested in particular concepts. This is a natural component of the process. It's occurring once more. Some people can detect when their ideas shift. "When I'm high, I always start thinking that way."

This can be a crucial step in preventing a full-blown manic episode from occurring.

Mania and hypomania both have cognitive symptoms.

People or things can distinctly influence someone's thinking when they are seen in a different light and when new ideas emerge in both quantity and quality. This might indicate that a mental episode is about to begin requiring action to prevent the symptoms from worsening.

Optimism and grandiosity have improved.

People who are manic or hypomanic often have an extremely optimistic outlook about themselves and the world around them. When people become manic, they frequently feel quite confident and well-adjusted. They commonly have beliefs that cause them to overestimate their skills, believe the world is a nice place, or underestimate the negative implications of their acts, all of which can lead to unpleasant feelings. The person's self-assurance can occasionally grow so strong that their thoughts become extravagant and misleading.

When people are manic or hypomanic, they may have a lot of fresh ideas and intentions. These plans and concepts frequently come to fruition. Unfortunately, it may be difficult to distinguish between excellent or harmful ideas when people are manic. When someone is having a manic episode, it's usual for them to have problems focusing and sticking to their goals (particularly when they are overactive or not sleeping much). Even the most brilliant ideas might fall flat if they aren't well-considered.

People may not assess the repercussions of their behavior during a manic or hypomanic episode. There is a tendency to rush into an activity or make a choice without first considering the benefits and drawbacks. They may also be so happy that they fail to think about any negative repercussions.

Many people believe they possess exceptional abilities, particularly when it comes to creativity and interpersonal interactions. People often only look at things that support their ideas, ignore things that don't. This can keep their faulty beliefs alive.

Paranoia

Paranoid thinking frequently occurs early on in bouts of mania or hypomania, and it can make individuals suspicious of one another. Often, this suspicion is founded on actual incidents and a history of unpleasantness between the patient and the distrusted person. Focusing on evidence that supports paranoid notions maintains the paranoia. Interactions with the other person are likely to be tense due to the high level of mistrust. The tension and hatred that come with it could cause the targeted individual to respond, and the patient could see this as confirmation of their paranoia.

An increased flow of thoughts

When people are manic or hypomanic, they frequently have a lot of new ideas and a desire to do many new activities. People who suffer from hypomanic symptoms often overestimate how much they can do in a day and underestimate how long things take to complete. Although, this isn't always the case. Maniacs have more activity in their heads, making it even more difficult for them to finish what they've started.

Errors in reasoning

When you're in hypomania, it's difficult to make appropriate social judgments, and it's even more difficult when you're manic. When persons with bipolar disorder engage with others, they generally have a reduced sense of self-awareness. They may say or do things out of character or fail to consider how their words or actions affect others, which can be harmful.

It's known as the Cognitive Behavioral Approach to mania prevention.

The following stages are included in the cognitive behavioral approach to addressing the cognitive and behavioral alterations that occur when someone is maniac or hypomanic:

1. Detecting emotional, cognitive, and behavioral changes early enough to assist.

2. Part of this involves changing inaccurate or harmful attitudes and beliefs or concepts like suspicion or grandiosity.

This is the third phase in planning and arranging activities, thoughts, or goals to keep them from becoming too distracting or overpowering.

In this section, we'll look at how you can learn to manage your thoughts so you don't spiral into mania. You need to be able to recognize what types of ideas you're having when you're high. When you're in a good mood, excessively optimistic ideas cannot be healthy for you because they'll make your mood even better. When you're in a good mood, overly happy ideas are considered detrimental, just as negative thoughts are when you're down.

There is a worksheet called "The Balance Sheet" On the following pages, accompanied by an example. It's a worksheet where you can jot down your overly happy ideas when you're in a good mood. Make a list of them just to be safe. In certain circumstances, your ideas may appear to be incredibly large, unlike how you usually think about things.

These ideas may not be of any assistance to you and may perhaps make matters worse. The second stage is to develop a more balanced thinking to replace the unhelpful one and then act on it.

The following are some questions you might ask yourself to help you think more clearly about things:

- Is it possible for me to demonstrate that my beliefs are correct?
- What facts or details may I have overlooked or failed to notice?

It's critical to inquire:

- Are there any alternative perspectives on what's going on?
- What would I think if I wasn't feeling well?
- What is a reasonable perspective on this?

This exercise may be quite effective if you practice it before you start to feel euphoric. Remember the best way to avoid a full-blown mania attack is to recognize the warning signals as soon as possible and take action before they worsen. When a person is experiencing a full-fledged manic episode, Cognitive Behavioral Therapy may not be effective. This is why it's critical to watch for early indicators of mania.

The Balance Sheet

Happy Ideas	More Balanced Thinking
Example: I'm going to get promoted today and get a huge pay rise	I'm doing well at work and need to discuss progression with my boss and the possibility of an increase in pay

Module 7: Behavioral Interventions to Prevent Mania

When a person begins to experience hypomania and mania, one of the indicators of bipolar illness is how their behavior alters. The time you spend sleeping decreases as your activity and libido increase. This pattern of increased activity and decreased sleep (or physical rest) can prolong and worsen mania.

Most of the time, these variations in activity levels begin small and gradually increase. Activity levels can be used to measure changes in mood in this way. It's critical to monitor your exercise levels when you begin to feel better. If your activity levels continue to rise, you should employ early intervention tactics to prevent a full-blown episode of mania. As part of your early intervention strategy, consider the following two options.

Aim: Keeping Sleep Disruptions at Bay

Sleep deprivation has been shown in several studies to both cause and be a symptom of mania. Some people become fatigued when they get little or no sleep, but they can't calm down sufficiently to fall asleep. These signs and symptoms might lead to a full-blown mania or even psychosis. Some may like the increased energy and vigor. Other bipolar patients may feel that this level of activity and energy is insufficient to keep them from becoming furious or paranoid.

Avoiding sleep difficulties is the best approach to cope with them. If feasible, attempt to predict when your typical sleeping patterns may be disrupted (e.g., when having to rush for a deadline, traveling, going on holidays, etc.)

Here are some ideal sleeping habits to maintain in order to avoid a hypomanic or manic episode:

- Going to bed and getting up at the same time every day. If you find that napping makes you tired at night, don't nap for too long or at all (e.g., share night-time responsibilities, bring your favorite pillow on holiday, use ear plugs or eye shields, or medications)
- Make sure you're not overstimulated (e.g., too much activity before bedtime, coffee) or that you're not thinking too much at night (do some relaxation exercises or calming activities)

Limiting your activities

Apart from medicine, there are a few things you may take to prevent mild or moderate mood swings from becoming a full-blown manic episode. People who want to avoid mania by adjusting their behavior should limit their activities and maintain a "normal" activity level. It's a good idea to plan and arrange your usual week using a Weekly Activity Schedule (available on the following page), making sure there's enough time for work, enjoyment, sleep and relaxation. When you suspect you're hypomanic, create a separate activity schedule to track your activity levels and compare them to your "normal" and "balanced" plan. If you discover that your activity levels have increased significantly, attempt to calm down and return to your routine. You might also enlist the assistance of a friend or family member.

So, keep it in mind...

The best techniques to avoid slipping into mania are to get adequate sleep and relax. What you should do are things that you can do fast after you see some of your early warning indicators. If you start to feel nervous or excited, there are numerous things you may do, such as go for a quiet and soothing walk in a lovely spot or take a lengthy bath. These techniques aren't designed to make you unhappy. They're meant to keep your high mood from escalating into mania. Many bipolar patients say they enjoy it when their mood improves, but they despise the full-fledged mania that comes with it. This is where you'll learn how to manage your moods so they don't spiral out of control.

Organizing and Prioritizing Projects and Ideas

When people are manic or hypomanic, they frequently have a lot of new ideas and desire to do a lot of new activities. People who suffer from hypomanic symptoms sometimes overestimate how much they can do in a single day. They don't consider how long it takes to complete tasks or how much it costs to put particular ideas into action.

Patients who are more upbeat and confident may take on too many initiatives, making it more likely they will not complete them or they will not exercise. They also face the danger of becoming exhausted from juggling too many tasks.

When you see your mood is improving and you're coming up with many creative ideas, it's time to start categorizing and assessing them. This exercise has a purpose. It's designed to assist you in slowing down and taking your time. You'll be able to keep track of your ideas and be more likely to complete some of these tasks, no matter how big or small if you write them down. Before you begin working on anything, you should consider several key factors. The activity 'Organizing Your Ideas List' may be done using the worksheet on the following pages.

The first thing to do is jot down all the activities or tasks you have in mind. Consider, "What are the expenses and advantages of putting these ideas into action?" Determine how much it will cost and how much it will benefit you to try this idea, project, job, or activity. Ask yourself, "What am I supposed to do now?"

Steps: What do I need to do to make my idea/project a success?

You must do this for every idea, project, new responsibility, or new action that comes to mind right now. Put your thoughts in the order you believe is best after you've given them some thought. As a result, you might wish to set a deadline for any idea or project you have. Execute the project or idea that you prioritized. Always keep in mind that you must complete the previous project or concept before beginning a new one. In this manner, you may keep your activity levels low while concentrating your attention and resources on one key job at a time, increasing your chances of success. It can also help you prevent a full-fledged manic episode, which might result in hospitalization, weariness, and a great deal of worry.

This exercise will help you to slow down. You'll keep track of all your innovative and interesting ideas and make sure at least some of them will come to fruition.

Organizing the ideas list

List of Ideas and Actions

Evaluating New Ideas and Actions

Costs

Benefits

Resources _____

Specific steps _____

Prioritized List of Ideas and Actions

When you evaluate a number of ideas and actions, list them in order of priority. At the same time, set a deadline for yourself regarding when each idea/action should be completed

Ideas or Actions in order of Priority

Deadline for Completion

_____

_____

Module 8: Self-Management and coping with psychosocial stressors

People with bipolar illness may be more prone to have symptoms if they experience stressful events in their lives, and they may be able to manage their stress to avoid depression and manic episodes. People with bipolar disorder may have difficulties with their families, careers, health, finances, and other aspects of their lives. One way to reduce stress is learning how to cope with challenges that arise regularly.

Some signals indicate what you should do.

The first step in identifying and recognizing issues is to acknowledge they exist. Several internal and external indicators might help you to recognize difficulties when they occur. Internal signals include physical changes in the body, such as tense muscles, headaches, breathing disturbances, and tightness in the chest. These bodily changes can be symptoms of stress and a means to determine whether there are any unresolved issues. Hopelessness, anxiety, and concern can all be signs that something is wrong in your life. Other people's actions might also help you figure out if there are issues. Family members, friends, and significant others are typically keen observers who can spot problems before the individual in question does.

It turns out that accepting other people's ideas or critiques, especially if they are seen as negative, can be difficult. Other people's comments can be unreasonable at times, but they can also be valuable since they indicate something is wrong.

Identifying and organizing problems

People with bipolar illness are more prone to suffer a slew of issues following a manic or depressive episode. Depression, for example, might make you drained and unmotivated, which can lead to losing your job. People who spend too much money and make poor financial judgments after a manic episode can wind up with debts they must repay. Feelings of rage and frustration can make it difficult to solve problems or even find out where to begin.

Having a clear system for identifying and dealing with problems as they arise might help alleviate feelings of hopelessness and overwhelm. As a result, if it's evident that there are issues, it's critical to take the following steps.

1. Divide the issues into categories.

People frequently have many issues, and it is difficult to determine which one requires immediate treatment. To begin problem-solving, choose a few issues to focus on and start with the most urgent or significant ones. There are various methods to achieve this, but one effective one is to write a list of anything consuming a lot of your time and energy lately (e.g., over the past week). The next step is to sort the things on the list by how much they drain your strength. Then, rank the issues according to their importance or urgency. The most significant and pressing problems should, in theory, receive the most attention. The reason this isn't occurring is you're spending a lot of time and energy on things that aren't as essential or urgent as they should be. This time and energy might be better spent on more important of urgent things. Problems that are most significant or urgent should be dealt with first.

2. Locate Supportive Resources for Coping

Coping resources are items that you or the environment may utilize to assist you in addressing the issues you've recognized.

Other people's aid, such as your family, friends, therapists, and coworkers, are examples of external resources. External resources can also include support services and organizations, money, transportation, and other natural resources that can assist those who are experiencing difficulties. To cope with stress, you can draw on internal coping skills such as assertiveness, intellect, and a sense of humor. Time, organization, resourcefulness, originality, confidence, and the capacity to ask for and accept aid from others are also necessary.

3. Look for items that make it difficult to cope.

Internal and external circumstances can make dealing with difficulties a challenge. That's why it's critical to understand what can be a problem to avoid it to the greatest extent feasible. External hurdles to successful issue resolution include a lack of knowledge about the problem, a lack of time, unpredictable schedules, deadlines, other commitments, and a lack of resources (e.g., money, work). Internal impediments might include a lack of answers to the problem, symptoms of mania or depression, or harmful ideas about the situation and your capacity to address it.

4. Address and remove impediments to effective coping.

It's critical to address any harmful attitudes or beliefs you have about your circumstance as soon as you identify what's preventing you from coping successfully. Always remember that asking for help or advice from others is perfectly acceptable.

Resources for Coping Worksheet

Things that could make you anxious, things that have made you stressed recently, or things you expect to worsen your stress can all be written down (remember, positive events may be stressful as well). Then, in the 'Coping Resources' column, list your talents and abilities. These might aid you in resolving issues. Consider how you may seek assistance from others, such as friends, family, your doctor, and so on. Then, look for items that can make it difficult for you to cope.

These obstacles might be internal, such as beliefs and attitudes, or external, such as unemployment, a large workload, or tight deadlines. How can you get beyond these stumbling blocks? When you do this, remember the tactics we discussed in previous sections. The last column is this one. You should make a note of these.

Psychosocial Problems & Stressors	Coping Resources	Barriers to effective coping	Strategies for overcoming barriers
Current:			
Recent Past:			
Future:			

Dealing with the problems alone isn't always enough. They must be resolved, and that is what we do. The majority of individuals work on difficulties daily. Many of the little decisions made every day are automatic. When deciding whether to get out of bed now or stay in bed for another 10 minutes, there are many options, risks, and rewards to consider. Larger issues are handled in the same way. For example, "I have a lot of stuff I need to get done before the end of the week," and "How am I going to finish them all on time?" After considering all the options, one is picked and implemented. If it doesn't work out, consider a new strategy instead. Problem solvers can recognize issues, weigh alternatives, make judgments, and devise a plan. There are instances when going through a step-by-step procedure to identify problems, develop solutions, and implement them can make the problem-solving process less intimidating.

The following is a step-by-step guide to assist individuals in solving their challenges.

1. Identifying and characterizing the issue

In this situation, I won't be able to pay my phone and gas bills this month due to a lack of funds.

2. Make a list of potential solutions.

At this time, don't be concerned with the solution's quality. Try to come up with at least 15 ideas without worrying about their quality. You could come up with some ideas you wouldn't have thought of otherwise if you let yourself be creative.

In the following stage, you'll look over each alternative and eliminate any that are less desired or unrealistic. Then, in order of desire, arrange the remaining options. You'll also consider the remaining options in terms of benefits and drawbacks.

4. The fourth phase entails devising a solution.

When and where will the solution be used? Call a gas provider tomorrow morning and try to work out a bargain to pay the gas bill next month.

- Who will take the initiative?
- How will the solution be put into action?
- When will the solution be implemented?

The next stage is to carry out your plans.

It's time to assess how effective the remedy was. Consider whether the current plan needs to be modified or a new plan is required to better address the situation.

Determine and characterize the problem area or issue first.

Be impartial and detailed in your description of the situation; don't express it in terms of your sentiments. Rather than focusing on what created the problem, try to determine what is preventing it from becoming better. Set objectives that are both reachable and realistic.

Problem Definition	Maintaining Factors	Goals for Problem Resolution

2. Generate possible solutions

❑ List all possible solutions without evaluating their quality or feasibility

❑ Eliminate less desirable or unreasonable solutions only after as many possible solutions have been listed

❑ Bearing in mind your goals for problem resolution, list the remaining solutions in order of preference

Preferred solutions	
1	
2	
3	
4	
5	
6	

3. Evaluate Alternatives

- Evaluate top 3 or 4 solutions in terms of their pros and cons

	Advantages	Disadvantages
Potential solution #1		
Potential solution #2		
Potential solution #3		
Potential solution #4		

4. Decide on a solution

❑ Decide on one or two solutions
❑ Specify actions and who will take action
❑ Specify how and when the solution will be implemented

Action Steps	Who	When

5. Implement Solution

❑ Implement the solution as planned.

6. Evaluate the Outcome

❑ Evaluate the effectiveness of the solution.

❑ Decide whether a revision of the existing plan or a new plan is needed to address the problem better.

Self-discipline

Congratulations! You've made it to the conclusion of this informational package! Congratulations on reading and working through all of the modules in order. If not, we recommend that you go back and review anything you might have missed. Most importantly, you should start putting some of your plans into action and continue to practice what you've learned or worked through! This implies that you must continue to apply all of the valuable abilities and insights about yourself that you've gained as a result of this knowledge. As a result, the concepts and techniques you've learned might begin to feel more like habits that fit into your daily routine.

It is recommended you keep a 'Self-Management Plan' that summarizes all of the relevant areas from these chapters that you want to address and how you plan to address them. Keep it close at hand so you can refer to it as needed. You might also wish to give a copy to a close family member or acquaintance. There will be ups and downs, just as in life. Here are some key points to keep in mind if you want to keep the gains you've achieved while going through this information package:

Expect Mistakes: Mistakes can happen at any moment and should be expected. It's important not to fall into the trap of thinking you're back to square one since this will only make you feel worse. When this circumstance arises, use your ability to test your ideas to assist you. Remember everyone has "bad days," or days when life's annoyances are more difficult to deal with — it's all part of being human! You can also use setbacks to learn something new about yourself to prevent repeating the same mistakes in the future.

Social Support: It's a good idea to find someone you can sit and talk to. This doesn't imply a therapy session where you pour your heart out but rather an opportunity to chat about what's going on in your life. This is a chance to discuss your goals and vent with someone you trust. It's well known that social support is an important factor in avoiding relapse. When a person attempts to solve an issue themselves, it can appear larger than it is. Hearing yourself speak about a situation may help you put it in context.

Relapse and episode recurrence are common in bipolar individuals, according to research. However, research has shown that sticking to your drug regimen and seeing your doctor or mental health practitioner regularly, as well as keeping an eye out for early warning symptoms and intervening early, can help you avoid being seriously ill.

Plan for Self-Management

- What are the telltale symptoms that I'm becoming sick (depressed or manic) and need to seek help?
- I'm not sure what I can do to keep myself from becoming sick.
- What conditions may be problematic for me?
- What may my friends and/or family say to me if I start to feel unwell?
- What am I supposed to say in response to what they say?
- What strategies/techniques have I discovered to be the most effective and would continue to use?

Thought Management:

Common unhelpful thoughts when my mood is depressed	What can I say to myself in response (balanced thoughts)

Common unhelpful thoughts when my mood is elevated	What can I say to myself in response (balanced thoughts)

What are my support options?

GP/Psychiatrist:

Counsellor/Agencies:

Friends:

Family:

Other:

Summary

- Bipolar disorder affects around 1% of the population, and it causes people to feel both joyful and depressed at the same time.

- This is known as a depressed episode or a hypomanic/manic episode.

- Bipolar 1 Disorder, Bipolar 2 Disorder, and Cyclothymic Disorder are the three types of bipolar disorder.

- Stressful life experiences can have a significant impact on the development of symptoms in bipolar patients.

- With increased confidence and optimism, there are strategies to reduce the incidence of depressed or manic episodes.

- It is critical to be aware of warning indications or cues that something is awry, as well as to be able to recognize and characterize them.

- Having a clear system in place for identifying and dealing with problems as they arise might help alleviate the feeling of hopelessness and overwhelm that comes with not knowing what to do.

- Make a list of the issues you want to address first, and then seek solutions to them.

CHAPTER 5

ANGER

WORKBOOK - CBT FOR ANGER MANAGEMENT

Overview of the Module Summary

Module 1: An overview of anger

Module 2: Techniques for controlling your rage

Module 1: An Overview of Anger

We all get furious from time to time. You should avoid doing anything severe, at the incorrect moment, or for an extended time. Anger might be a simple irritation with something, or it can be an indication of rage. It can also result in furious shouting, screaming, and lashing out on the other end of the spectrum. Anger may sometimes be harmful to our relationships and our jobs. It can also alter our perceptions of ourselves. Angry people may attribute their rage to other people or a specific scenario. When individuals are let down in any manner or aren't given something they believe they should have, they become enraged.

When your body is worried, fearful, or nervous, physical reactions occur. This is known as the "fight or flight" reaction. This response occurs swiftly and aids in the body's preparation for action. We learn how to defend ourselves against danger or run from it.

- Increasing our heart rate so more blood can reach our muscles. This is exactly what we need to accomplish.
- Increasing our sweat production to keep us cool.

We're preparing our muscles for action at this stage.

- Deeper and faster breathing to provide oxygen to our muscles.

When you don't require certain physiological functions, such as digestion, you can turn them off.

- Racing thoughts: determining the best actions and making a speedy decision.

This would have provided us with some protection in the past. It helped us stay alive and move fast if there were predators while we hunted and gathered food. We don't have to run or fight as much as we used to in order to solve difficulties these days. On the other hand, the symptoms listed above aren't really helpful. Is it even feasible to do so? There is no need to become enraged when faced with threats such as money problems, work problems, unhelpful employees, rude drivers, or people who refuse to assist you. These signs and symptoms aren't harmful on their own. It's a good answer in many respects but it's given at the wrong moment. We don't need to be terrified of the fight or flight reaction to avoid it. It is the healthy defense system for our bodies. Knowing this can make dealing with physical symptoms easier. Do not be concerned about them or feel obligated to respond or react. They don't need to know that you're concerned about them. You can let them go because they'll be gone in no time.

What causes you to be angry?

The causes differ from person to person and situation to situation. They also change regularly.

Your body changes when you're angry.

Energy is made by your body when you're angry.

Here's how it works:

- Adrenaline and other chemicals get into your bloodstream.
- The heart pumps faster.
- Blood moves faster.
- Your muscles become tight.

Everyone gets angry at some point. If you learn how to deal with anger well, you can overcome problems and feel better about yourself.

The problem is when you get angry too much or if you get angry in the wrong way.

Examples might be when you have trouble with family and friends, or work, or legal and financial issues.

Some common things that make people angry:

Stress

Stress from work, family, health, and money problems can make you feel anxious and angry.

Frustration

Angry if you don't reach a goal or think things are out of your hands.

Fear

A natural reaction to threats of violence, physical or verbal abuse, or when someone is being mean to you is fear and anger.

Annoyance

You might get angry at small irritations and things that happen every day.

Disappointment

When expectations and desires aren't met, people can get angry.

Resentment

Angry feelings can happen when you have been hurt, rejected, or hurt.

There may be times in your life when you are more likely to get angry than others. You might be on high alert if you are exposed to a certain situation or place. For example, some people find that they are much more likely to get angry when they're driving.

There are different types of thinking styles. Our interpretation and thoughts about a situation can make us angry, especially when we think about other people's intentions and what that could mean for us. It can be very hard to deal with when we feel someone has wronged us. Also, when someone has done something we think is wrong. Our understanding of anger may also affect how we act. As we think about anger, we can change how we show or control our anger. For example, if we think anger shouldn't be "bottled up," it's possible we haven't thought about trying to manage our emotions more appropriately.

Behavioral Explanations: It might be hard for you to sit with and tolerate anger. This could be because of how you've lived your life. Also, what you have come to think is normal and acceptable. You may not have had the chance to learn how to better manage and express your emotions. Angry behavior can start to form into a habit. As time goes on, this can get more and more difficult to deal with. In reality, it is likely that a lot of these things make someone angry. However, in some ways, knowing what makes us angry isn't as important as knowing what stops us from moving on.

Anger is what keeps it going.

When someone is angry, there may be a clear pattern of what happens before and after they do something bad, such as driving, taking care of the kids, or talking about money.

There may be both costs and benefits to being angry. Anger can be good for short-term gains, but many people know it can also be detrimental. For example, getting what you want or having people treat you with respect is good. But, it can also cost a lot in the long run, such as a broken relationship. Consider these things for yourself and see if they make you want to change or if you need to do something.

At a deeper level, it's clear that our behavior, thoughts, and feelings, as well as our physical sensations, all work together to keep our anger problems going.

Module 2: Techniques for controlling your rage

Do the following:

Start by taking a break. Stop what you're doing and come back when you're calmer.

When you start to get angry, tell yourself to stop. This may help you calm down and think more clearly, but you should talk to your doctor first.

Try to let go.

Try counting to 10 or 100.

Take a sip of water.

Take a stroll.

Take a few slow, deep breaths.

Leave if you need to.

Angry people should know everyone needs a break. If you need someone to look after a child, an older person, or someone who is sick, you can ask them to do it. Then, go to a safe place where you can calm down. Don't get behind the wheel, please.

When you're calm, come back.

Talk to the person or face the situation that made you angry after you've cooled down.

Remember to be calm.

Take your time before you speak. The less you say, the less likely you'll say something you'll later be sorry about.

Name the problem.

Explain why you're angry or what the problem is in a calm and clear way. Don't yell, use insults, or make threats when you talk to someone. People won't be as likely to think about your point.

Use "I" statements instead of "you."

After you tell the person about the problem, use "I" statements to explain how you feel about it. These statements are all about you and what you want, need, and feel. They also help the person listening to not feel blamed or criticized.

Find solutions.

In the future, say what you'd like to change or see happen, and then say why. If you're in a fight with someone else, try to work things out together.

If you need help, ask for it.

If you can't show your anger in a healthy way, talk to a family member or friend. Or, speak to a counselor or other mental health professional. They can help you learn how to talk about your feelings through role-playing and other methods.

Avoid doing the following:

You might have a hard time getting over your anger. Painful events from a long time ago may be etched in your mind. As time goes on, your anger may grow. You might become obsessed with angry thoughts or the idea of getting back at the person who hurt you.

Putting it in a bottle

Most of the time, this will make you feel worse. Sooner or later, your emotions come out. People sometimes get angry when they don't get what they want. Angry feelings may also cause health problems if you keep them inside.

Blaming

There is no point in blaming other people for your problems. To be a good person, you need to learn to take responsibility for your own feelings and actions, both good and bad.

Responding to anger with anger is not the best way to deal with it.

This may seem like a natural thing to do, but it often makes things worse.

Alcohol and other drugs can make people more angry.

People who use alcohol or other drugs to get rid of their anger don't get any less angry. These substances may make you feel less angry for a short time, but only if you use them. In many cases, they don't work at all. There is a big role for alcohol and other drugs in a lot of violent crimes.

Practice positive self-talk

In the space below, write down a few things that made you angry. Did you tell yourself a bad thing? How would you tell yourself to be happy if the problem or situation came up again?

Situation

1. _____

2. _____

3. _____

Negative Message

1. _____

2. _____

3. _____

Positive Message

1. _____

2. _____

3. _____

Practice your 'I' statements

When you're angry, it's easy to point the finger at someone or something. Learning how to use "I" statements can help you become more aware of how you feel. Fill in the statements below to learn how to talk about yourself and your feelings.

Because I'm so angry, I don't want to talk to you.

When ___you are late for dinner,

For dinner, we will have _____

Next time, I want to know if you're going to be late.

Please call.

More ways to help yourself

Progressive muscle relaxation

When things start to get hot, try these ways to cool down:

Start at the top of your head and work your way down to your toes. This is how:

1. Wear clothes that are easy to move in. You can either sit in a chair or lie down.

2. Tense the muscles in your face for about five to ten seconds. Then, for about 20 seconds, let them go.

3. Tense the muscles in the back of your neck for about five to ten seconds, then let them go. Then, for about 20 seconds, let them go. Make sure you pay attention to how your muscles feel when you're calm.

4. Go to your shoulder. You should do the same thing as step 3.

Have a sense of humor

As a general rule, people who have a good sense of humor are less likely to get angry. You should try to find the humor in small problems and annoyances.

Do something you enjoy

Among other things, you could try gardening, learning to play a musical instrument, or making crafts. A hobby can be a good way to relieve stress and energy, and it can also be a good way to get away from angry feelings.

Write about how you feel

Keep a journal or write a letter (you don't have to send it) and write down your thoughts and feelings. Writing can help you improve your skills.

You can do this for each muscle group in your body, one at a time. For example, you can do this for your hands, arms, chest, etc.

Visualization

Use your imagination to help you relax and lessen your anger with this technique.

1. Sit in a chair or lay down

2. Imagine a lush forest or a sandy beach. These could be good places to think about. Is this where you want to be?

3. Look at the scene. Keep going until you feel refreshed and relaxed.

Understanding why you are angry

Look at some of these examples and see if you can add something from your own life. See if you can find a similar pattern in yourself.

Anger is a habit

As time goes on, anger can become a normal, familiar, and predictable response to a lot of different situations. When anger is shown often and aggressively, it can become a bad habit. A habit, by definition, is when you do the same thing over and over without thinking about it. People who show their anger continually should think of this as a bad habit because it causes problems.

- Do you get angry all the time? How?

- How has it not worked out well.

Breaking the habit of being angry

You can break the anger habit by becoming aware of the events and circumstances that make you angry and the bad things that happen after. In addition, you need to develop a set of effective ways to deal with your anger.

- Think of some ways to control your anger that you know or have used in the past.

Events and cues

People learn how to look at an angry situation in this class. This is about recognizing events and signs indicating that your anger is getting worse.

Events that make you angry

The reason why you get angry is because of your interpretation of events in your life. Many times, specific events touch on very important issues. These "red flags" or "sensitive areas" usually refer to things ongoing on for a long time, leading easily to anger. It's not just things happening now; we may also reflect on times in the past that made us angry. When you think about these past events, you might get angry.

Angry people can get angry at these things:

- Waiting for a long time on the phone or in an office
- Being stuck in traffic or on a crowded bus or having to clean up someone else's mess
- A friend not paying back money that they owe you
- Neighbors who are inconsiderate
- Dealing with a frustrating person or situation on the Internet

What are some of the things that make you angry?

What are some of the things and events that make you angry?

Types of cues:

Another important way to keep track of your anger is to look for the signs that come up after an anger-related event. These signs show that you've become angry and that your anger is getting worse. There are four types of cues: physical, behavioral, emotional, and cognitive (or thought) cues, each of which can be broken down into two groups: physical and behavioral. Every time you get angry, write down the things that happen in each category and what you notice.

–   Physical cues (how your heart rate goes up, your chest gets tight, or you get hot or flushed.
–   Behavioral cues (what you do, such as clenching your fists, raising your voice, or staring at other people)
–   Emotional cues (other feelings like fear, hurt, jealousy, or disrespect) that can happen with anger.
–   Cognitive Cues (what you think about when you think about the event, such as hostile self-talk, images of aggression, and revenge) are also important.

Check-in: Monitoring anger for the week

In this session, you will learn how to keep track of your anger and recognize your anger-related events and situations. Monitoring your anger will help you become more aware of your anger patterns and the situations, thoughts, feelings, and consequences linked to that anger. There will be a check-in procedure in each weekly session. It will be used to follow up on the between-session challenge from the previous week and to report the highest level of anger reached on the anger meter during the last week. You will also use the anger awareness record to write down the event that made you angry, the cues that made you angry, the positive or negative consequences, and the strategies you used to deal with your anger after the event. Every time you start a new class, you'll use the following format to check in.

1. In the last week, how angry were you?

2. What made you angry?

3. What cues were associated with the anger-related event?

Physical cues

Behavioral cues

Emotional cues

Cognitive cues

4. What did you do to keep your anger level from getting to 10?

_____

_____

_____

For each day of the upcoming week, monitor and record the highest number you can reach on the anger meter:

____M ____T ____W ____Th ____Fri ____Sat ____Sun

Events, cues, and strategies identified during the check-in Procedure

Event ➝	Cues ➝	Strategies

Anger-control plans

In this session, you will learn specific ways to deal with your anger. This is the list of things you'll do to keep your anger in check.

A plan to control your anger

There has been a lot of talk about how to keep track of how angry you are with the group. We talked about how to use an anger meter in our first class. You learned how to figure out what caused you to be angry, and the physical, behavioral, emotional, and cognitive cues of each event. You also learned how to keep track of things like events, cues, outcomes, and strategies with the anger record.

In this session, you will learn how to control your anger with timeouts and relaxation. You will also work on developing your own anger control plans. These plans are called "toolboxes," and the specific ways they control anger are called "tools."

There should be both immediate and preventive strategies in a good set of tools to control your anger. Timeouts, deep-breathing exercises, and stopping your thoughts are some examples of immediate methods. Examples of ways to avoid getting sick are to start an exercise program and to change your irrational beliefs. These strategies will be talked about in later classes.

Timeouts

The timeout is a simple way to deal with anger that should be in everyone's plan. There are times when you might get angry and need to take a break, just like there are times when you might need to take a break in sports. You can start by taking a few deep breaths and not reacting right away. It could also mean leaving the situation that is making you angry or just stopping the conversation that is making you angry.

It's possible to make a formal timeout policy that affects your relationships with your family, friends, and coworkers. This is the formal way to use a timeout. It means that there must be an agreement, or a plan in place, that any of the people involved can call a timeout and that all of them agreed to in advance. Calling a timeout doesn't mean that you have to leave the situation unless you need to. But it's agreed you will come back to finish the discussion or put it off, depending on whether the people involved think they can solve the problem.

Even if a person's anger is rising quickly on the anger meter, they can still avoid reaching ten by taking a break and leaving the situation. A timeout is also good when used with other strategies. Among other things, you can take a break and go for a walk. Also, you can take a break and call a friend or family member you trust. You can also write in your journal. These other things help you calm down during your timeout.

When you need help from other people, you can ask.

An important part of your plan to control your anger could be getting help from friends and family. We all need help at different times in our lives to reach our goals and deal with problems that come our way. It can be very helpful to have a group of people who understand and support your desire to change. You could ask for help and advice from family and friends, as well as members of 12-step groups, 12-step sponsors, or members of other mutual help groups, to help you get through this. A social support action plan you write up on your own may help you stay on track when you want support.

Plan for getting help

Plan for Seeking Support

Support	How this support will help	Plan for getting this support

Support	How this support will help	Plan for getting this support
Support	How this support will help	Plan for getting this support

- Can you think of a person you could ask for help with your social life? How would you ask them to help you?
- The timeout strategy can be used in a lot of different ways. Please explain them.
- Can you think of specific ways that you might try to keep your anger in check? Please explain them.

The following is a sample of a plan to control your anger:

1. Take some time off.

2. Talk with a friend (someone you trust).

3. Use the Conflict Resolution Model to solve problems with expressing anger (the one we talked about).

4. Work out (for example, take a walk or go to the gym).

5. Find out what is going on inside you that isn't anger.

Breathing aids relaxation

As a way to unwind, we'll close this session with a deep breathing exercise. Pay attention to your breathing, take a few deep breaths, and attempt to let go of any tension in your body to execute this exercise on your own. You should repeat this as often and as long as possible. The steps are as follows.

Find a comfy area to sit in your chair. Close your eyes if you want to. If not, simply glance at the ground. Take a moment to relax. Pay close attention to your body now. Start with your feet and work your way up to your head, looking for symptoms of tension along the way. Pay attention to how you move and notice any tightness in your legs, stomach, hands and arms, shoulders, neck, and face. Try to relax and let go of any tension. Pay attention to your breathing now. Inhale and exhale slowly. You may find this a really relaxing activity.

Take a deep breath and hold it. Take note of how your lungs and chest are expanding. Now, take a deep breath. Breathe deeply once again. Inhale deeply into your lungs and chest. It's best if you can get as much fresh air as possible. Take time to think about it. Now, let go of it and breathe softly. Inhale softly and deeply one more time. Hold it for a second before releasing it.

Continue to breathe in this manner for a few minutes longer. Continue to focus on your breathing. With each inhale and exhale, feel your body getting more relaxed. To relieve any leftover tension, use your breath.

Take a big breath now. Inhale deeply, hold for a second, and then exhale slowly. Continue to pay attention to your breath as it fills your lungs and how it feels by inhaling, holding, and then letting go. When you do this again, take a deep breath in, hold it for a second, and then exhale slowly.

Open your eyes when you're ready. How did it go? Did you notice anything new when you inhaled? What are your current feelings?

You only need to do three deep inhalations and three deep exhalations to complete this breathing exercise. It can help you relax even if you don't do anything else while your anger worsens. This is something you can do anywhere. At home, at work, on the bus, waiting for an appointment, or even walking. Deep breathing is most effective as a relaxation method when used frequently and in various contexts.

Reorganization of the mind

The A-B-C-D Model, a means to shift your thinking, will be discussed in this session. You'll also learn about thought pausing, a different way of considering things.

The A-B-C-D Model is a method of thinking about how things operate.

The A-B-C-D Model corresponds to some people's perceptions of anger management treatment. The letter "A" stands for an event that starts things up in this model. The "event," sometimes known as a "red-flag incident," is what kicks everything off. "B" represents our thoughts on the event that prompted us to begin. Our perceptions and opinions about the events make us upset, not the facts themselves. The letter "C" expresses how this scenario makes you feel. These emotions arise from differing perspectives and opinions about what occurred. If there is a question, it is denoted with a "D." This section of the model focuses on recognizing any erroneous ideas and refuting them using more reasonable or realistic perspectives on the incident that led to them. This is how you should replace self-defeating comments that upset or aggravate your anger with concepts that help you think more realistically and properly about what happened.

- What does each letter of the A-B-C-D Model mean, and how do they all work together?

_____

_____

_____

- List some of your bad ideas.

_____

_____

_____

There are some things you could say to disagree with these ideas.

_____

_____

_____

The A-B-C-D Model is a way to think about how things work.

A means starting a situation or event that is going to happen.

As you know, **B** stands for Belief System.

- What you think about the event (your self-talk).
- What you think and expect of other people.

C stands for Consequence.

–   How you think about the event based on your own self-talk

D is disputing the facts.

–   Examine your beliefs and expectations
–   Are they unrealistic or not very useful?

The thought-stopping approach

The second approach is called "thought stopping." This is a second way to control your anger. If you want to stop thinking about something, you can do this. In this method, you tell yourself through a series of self-commands to stop thinking about the things that make you angry, and then you do it. I need to stop thinking these thoughts; if I keep thinking this way, I will only get into trouble. You might say, "Don't buy into this situation," or, "Don't go to that place." To put it another way, instead of trying to argue with your thoughts and beliefs, as in the A-B-C-D Model above, the goal is to stop your current pattern of angry thoughts before they lead to more anger and a loss of control.

What are some other examples of thought-stopping statements to use when you become angry?

Challenging unhelpful thoughts

Think about things in differently, and you'll be more stressed and in a bad mood. Many of these thoughts happen outside our control, and can be bad or unhelpful. When you think about these things, remember they are just your ideas and don't have to be true. Many unhelpful thoughts are true when we are angry. But these should be questioned because they are often based on wrong assumptions. This is important to remember.

The next part will help you see if your thoughts are unhelpful or unrealistic and how you can change this. People who do this can learn to see things in a more realistic way, which can improve their mood and help them deal with their anger. You might think about all kinds of things in an unhelpful way.

As a start, here are some examples:

The following is about you and what you do and think:

- I have the right to some things.
- I must stand up for myself.
- I can't stand being annoyed.

About other people:

- Everybody is out to get me.
- Nobody is on my side.
- There is always someone to blame.

About anger:

- I have to talk about how angry I am.
- It's not a good idea to keep this strong feeling inside of you.

People who think this way might become angrier. There are ways to think shown above. Do you think of any of them?

Now, it is time to add your examples.

_____

_____

_____

_____

_____

_____

You might have a hard time figuring out which thought isn't good for you. Then try to remember when you were angry. At that time, think about what was on your mind.

Patterns of unhelpful thinking

There are a lot of bad thoughts you need to be able to spot at the start. Then, you can fight back. Being aware of the common patterns that unhelpful thoughts follow can help you recognize when you have them. This will make it easier for you to stop them.

The following are some of the most common ways that our unhelpful thoughts go about their business:

- Figuring out what will happen in the future
- Catastrophizing
- What would happen?

When people are worried about something, they often spend a lot of time thinking about it. Youthink about the future and what could go wrong. Instead of leaving things as they are you may think things are worse or you think there will be a bad event.

As an example:

- What if they don't like me?
- What if I lose all my friends?

Here, you are jumping to conclusions, taking things personally, seeing things as your own, or mind reading.

There's a good chance when people are feeling vulnerable, they take things personally and pay more attention to what people say to them. Sometimes, they can be too quick to draw conclusions and think they are the main point of what has been said.

As an example:

- It was not an accident.

- They must think I'm a fool.

Here you focus on the bad, neglecting the good things, or filtering.

Often, people don't pay attention to the good things in their lives, or their situation. Instead, we focus on the things that are bad. When we think this way, we don't feel good about ourselves. It can make you less confident.

As an example:

- My kids are a mess, no matter how well they played with each other before.

Here, you are thinking in black and white; it's either all or nothing, focusing on perfectionism, or you are 'should' thinking.

People sometimes only see things in black and white, with no gray area or middle ground. Having this polarized view can lead some people to set unrealistic standards for themselves, be too critical, and not be able to see any progress because of their perfectionism.

As an example:

- That was a waste of time.
- They must not like me.
- I should always get 100%.

Here, you are over-generalizing and labelling.

Based on one single event, you might think that other events will follow the same pattern in the future. You might not be able to see a bad event as just one. This can also mean you call yourself names that aren't very nice, making you feel bad and even hopeless.

As an example:

- In other words, if I fail my driving test, I'll fail at everything I do.
- All dogs are mean because he barked at me
- I can't do anything.

If so, do any of your unhelpful thoughts fit into any of these patterns? Is there anything that comes to mind? Make a note of it in the box below:

Unhelpful thought	Category

We can learn ways to fight against these thoughts that aren't good for us. Improve your mood and deal with your angry feelings: This can help you do both of these things. The next part of this handout will talk about how we can change our unhelpful thoughts and how to do that. You may come up with a more balanced thought that is correct and based on facts.

How to challenge unhelpful thoughts

You need to challenge a thought once you know it isn't good for you. To do this, you can think about a lot of different things. Take a look at this:

Situation: Someone looks over at you when you're out with friends.

People describe how they feel in this way: Anxious.

A thought that isn't very useful: They think I'm dumb!

Challenges to a thought that isn't good

When you ask these questions, you can challenge your bad ideas.

If this is true, is there any evidence to back it up?

–   In the past, he hasn't talked to me. I haven't met him, either.

Can you think of any unhelpful thinking patterns I talked about earlier?

- I'm assuming too much.
- Mind-reading, too.
- Putting myself in a box.

If a friend had this thought, what would you say to them?

- I would say that you don't know what he's thinking or why he looked over at the door.

Why would it be bad or good for you to think this way?

- Costs: I'm going to be on edge a lot and be suspicious of other people because of this.
- I can't think of any.

In 6 months, how will you feel about this? I'm sure I'll look back and think how silly I was.

Is there another way to look at this?

- I don't know why he looked over there. It could be that he was looking for someone.

What do I need to do after I have asked myself these questions?

You should try to think of a more balanced or rational way to look at the subject. As an example:

People don't care why that person looked. Nobody should think that they thought I was bad. It doesn't mean I was being judged.

When you notice thoughts that aren't very helpful, try to think of ways to apply these questions to them. People who use it can improve their mood and learn how to deal with their angry feelings. You can use this method to see if your thoughts are real and balanced.

Identifying unhelpful thoughts

Whenever your mood changes, try to write down what you were doing, how you felt, and what you were thinking at the time.

Identifying Unhelpful Thoughts

Whenever your mood changes, try to write down what you were doing, how you felt, and what were thinking at the time. You might find that patterns begin to emerge.

Situation	Feelings	Thoughts

Challenging Unhelpful Thoughts

Taking a particularly unhelpful thought, see if you can test it.

Ask questions to test whether your belief has any real basis.

Unhelpful Thought

Challenges

Is there any evidence that contradicts this thought?

Can you identify any patterns of unhelpful thinking?

What would you say to a friend who had this thought in a similar situation?

What are the costs and benefits of thinking this way? Benefits: Costs:
How will you feel about this in 6 months time?
Is there another way of looking at this situation?

Training in assertiveness

Now we'll discuss assertiveness, the Conflict Resolution Model, and how acting assertively may assist you in resolving conflicts with others.

Being assertive is a learned skill.

Aggressive people conduct actions intending to injure or damage people or property. It is something you learned about in session 1. This might take the form of verbal abuse, threats, or physical violence. If someone does you wrong or treats you unfairly, the first thing you usually do is fight back. My feelings, opinions, and beliefs are all extremely important to me. It makes no difference to me what you think or feel.

Acting passively or non-aggressively is one approach to avoid becoming aggressive, but this is wrong; you've allowed your rights to be infringed upon. When individuals mistreat you, you could resent yourself for failing to safeguard your rights. You should be far more concerned about your feelings, opinions, and beliefs than I am.

A passive-aggressive person believes others are placing too many demands on them, so they refuse to comply or try to make matters worse. Saying you don't agree with the demand in an authoritative rather than passive-aggressive manner can help people comprehend your point of view. You might then be able to reach an agreement.

From an anger management standpoint, you should respond assertively when dealing with someone who wronged you. It entails sticking up for yourself while remaining respectful to others. Assertiveness communicates to people that their feelings, opinions, and views are equally significant to them. This is the most important point. You may talk about your feelings, ideas, and beliefs with the person who violated your rights if you behave assertively without coping with the unpleasant repercussions of aggressiveness or the depreciation of yourself that comes with being quiet or non-aggressive.

Forceful, aggressive, and passive answers are all taught behaviors, not inborn characteristics. You may learn to be more forceful when you encounter problems with others by following the Conflict Resolution Model. This will make it easier for you to cope with them.

- What happens if you respond aggressively when you disagree with someone else?

- What may happen if you don't fight back when things become heated?

- What are some of the advantages of assertiveness in problem-solving situations?

Conflict resolution model

This model can be used when you wish to take a firm stance. It consists of five easy-to-remember phases.

1. Determining the nature of the problem. This stage is all about determining the source of the dispute (like a friend not being on time when you come to pick them up).

2. We'll figure out how we feel in this phase. This phase involves determining how you feel about the conflict (for example, frustration, hurt, or annoyance).

3. Find out what kind of influence it had. This phase determines what the issue that is creating the conflict will entail (for example, being late for the meeting that you and your friend plan to attend).

4. Deciding whether or not to resolve the disagreement. This phase involves determining whether or not to resolve the disagreement. Do you believe it is significant enough to mention?

When, how, and when not to deal with and resolve conflict:

5. Make a day and time to discuss the dispute, express how you perceive it, discuss how you feel about it, and come up with a solution.

People who are enraged and their families

You'll reflect on how anger and other emotions were expressed in your own family in these two sessions. It's about examining how previous family relationships have influenced your current ideas, feelings, and behavior.

Anger and the family

Our interactions with our parents have had a significant influence on how we think, feel, and act as adults for many of us. Concerning rage and how we express it, our parents or other individuals who raised us generally modeled how we feel and react. In the next series of questions, we'll want to hear about your connections with your parents and the families you lived with when you were younger. Talking about family issues might make you feel horrible at times, but it's something you should discuss with a group leader or your counselor.

- Discuss your family. No, I didn't live with both of them at the same time. Are there any other members of your family? I'm at home.

How did your family express their displeasure with you as a child? What was your father's method of expressing his rage? What was your mother's method of expressing her rage? No, I haven't received any threats of violence. Was one parent cruel to the other or you?

- How did your family express other feelings to one another, such as happiness and sadness? Was the display of emotions restricted to anger and irritation, or did it include a wide range of emotions?
- Do you recall how and who did it? Was there any physical punishment (e.g., hitting with hands, belts, switches, or other objects)? What were your thoughts on this?
- How did you spend your childhood? Were you, among other things, a hero, a savior, a victim, a clown, a scapegoat, or something else?
- What did you learn about your father and males in general from your experience with him? What did you discover about your mother and other women as a result of your research?
- Is there anything you feel, think, or do today that impacts your relationships? What are these behaviors used for nowadays? What would happen if you put a stop to it?

Ending exercise

- What have you learned about how to deal with anger?

- Make a list of the ways you will try to control your anger. These strategies can help you better control your anger. How can you use these strategies?

- What can you do to keep improving your anger management skills, and how can you? Are there any areas that need to be worked on?

CHAPTER 6

SLEEP

WORKBOOK - CBT CAN HELP YOU SLEEP BETTER

Overview of the Module Summary

Module 1: Sleep's origins

Module 2: Your thoughts and insomnia

Module 1: Sleep's Origins

When we get a good night's sleep, our lives are so much better. Many of us don't think about it much. People typically notice and try to figure out how sleep works for the first time when they have sleep issues. Some species of fish and insects do not sleep (although they may rest). Humans sleep in a variety of ways, but they prefer to do it in extended blocks.

We are all familiar with the appearance of sleep. People who are sleeping close their eyes, lie down, breathe slowly, relax their muscles, and keep their bodies calm, but they may move their bodies from time to time. Getting to sleep is not the same as going into a coma or passing out. Loud noises, bright lights, or even touch can wake sleeping people.

The sleep phases

According to many studies, there are two forms of sleep: REM and non-REM sleep.

We fall asleep in REM rapid-eye-movement sleep around 25% of the time. Electrical activity in the brain, highly relaxed muscles, the body becoming motionless, and rapid eye movements as the eyes dart back and forth under closed eyelids characterize this form of sleep. REM sleep provides energy to the brain and body, which helps function during the day. Many individuals experience dreams when in REM sleep., However, they can occur at any time during the night.

When most people go to sleep, they don't move their eyes. "NREM" stands for "non-rapid-eye-movement sleep." It occurs around 75% of the time and may be divided into four stages:

In Stage 1, the person is between being awake and going to sleep. This is a light sleep state. Stage 2 is the beginning of sleep when the individual is no longer aware of what is going on around them. The body cools down, and breathing and heart rate become more consistent.

- Stages 3 and 4 are referred to as "delta sleep," the deepest and most restorative sleep period. Stage 3 serves as a bridge to Stage 4, often known as "true delta." Blood pressure drops, respiration slows, muscles relax and get more blood, tissue develops and heals, and hormones are produced during these stages (including growth hormone, which is why growing teenagers need to sleep more).

Sleep is necessary and beneficial

Sleep, like oxygen, water, and food, is essential for everyone. A person may spend a long time without sleep, but the longer they remain up, the more they desire to sleep.

For a long time, scientists have debated the precise purpose and function of sleep. Most people think that sleep is good for both the body and the mind. Delta sleep (stages 3 and 4) is considered vital for bodily restoration and physical energy. REM sleep is regarded as crucial for memory and attention.

A good night's sleep is vital for your overall physical health. It's essential for recovering from accidents or illnesses, and growing, and maintaining your psychological well-being and mood. It also aids focus, memory, work performance, and interpersonal relationships.

Consequences of little sleep

When it comes to sleep, everyone has various requirements. Adults obtain an average of 6-8 hours of sleep every night; however, some people may operate well with less sleep while others need more to complete their work. Sleep deprivation or poor sleep quality can have a variety of consequences, including:

- Irritability and other mood swings due to a lack of focus, attention, and memory.
- There will be issues with decision-making and reaction speed (dangerous for driving).

These consequences might be either harmful or good, depending on how bad the sleep deprivation is. This is determined by how long the sleep issues have been present and how significant the day's chores and obligations are. It's critical to get treatment if you're experiencing difficulties sleeping.

How well do those who get enough sleep perform?

Good sleepers usually fall asleep less than 30 minutes after the sun sets. During the night, they'll wake up once or twice. You won't be happy if you expect to fall asleep as soon as you go to bed or not wake up at all during the night. Even the world's finest sleepers wouldn't be able to accomplish this! The best sleepers will experience nights when falling asleep takes a long time. Stressful occurrences are often to blame. It normally disappears within a few days. People may also find it difficult to get back to sleep after waking up in the middle of the night.

When you can't sleep at night, you have insomnia.

There are several types of insomnia, but what exactly is it?

- Difficulty falling asleep - also known as onset insomnia
- Waking up in the middle of the night and not being able to return to sleep
- Waking up extremely early and not being able to get back to sleep

These are not the same as other sleep issues, such as being exhausted all the time, having nightmares, or sleepwalking.

Insomnia turns out to be the most frequent mental health issue. The condition affects 15% to 30% of the adult population, with women suffering from the condition twice as often as men. Insomnia is more common in older individuals than in younger people; however, it can affect people of all ages. Most individuals struggle with sleep at some time in their lives, but if you have persistent insomnia, you should get treatment. If you're having trouble sleeping even when you're not using sleeping pills, you should contact your doctor.

Insomnia is frequently connected to other mental health issues.

Insomnia has several causes.

There are several factors that may stop you from falling asleep. Some of these issues include:

- Pain
- Side effects of medication
- Caffeine, nicotine, extreme anxiety or despair, stressful events in your life, and daytime napping

These are just a few of the factors that might make it difficult to sleep. Sleep medications might also make it difficult to sleep.

Two factors could induce insomnia: one that starts it and another that keeps it going and makes it a long-term condition.

The insomnia cycle is a nightmare

People can become trapped in a cycle of insomnia, acquiring behaviors or attitudes that aid in the continuation of sleep issues even when triggered by something else. For instance, it was difficult to sleep initially due to stress, discomfort, or another factor.

Habits that should be followed

Some of the disorders that may occur are depression, generalized anxiety disorder, and post-traumatic stress disorder. People can underestimate the importance of insomnia because they believe it's only a sign of something else when, in reality, it may require treatment on its own.

Insomnia has a negative impact

Insomnia is a serious condition despite its prevalence. A long-term sleep problem can affect your ability to perform well both during the day and at night.

Things like napping or spending a lot of time in bed trying to sleep won't help. They make things worse because they only aggravate the situation.

It's easy to have negative ideas like, "I won't be able to cope if I don't get enough sleep," or "If I don't get enough sleep tomorrow, I'll feel horrible and won't be able to perform effectively at work."

Stress caused by a lack of sleep and tense muscles

Consider these:

• Poor memory and attention • Low mood or anger • Trouble staying awake • Fear of not sleeping • Poor work performance • Relationship conflict • Reduced quality of life

If any of these things happen to you because of a lack of sleep, you may need to seek assistance.

How to deal with insomnia

Insomniacs can take a variety of medications to help them sleep, but they typically only work for a limited time. People who have sleep problems could consider measures such as sleep hygiene, cognitive therapy, and stress reduction.

Module 2: Your Thoughts and Insomnia

Let's discuss the different types of insomnia in more depth.

Primary insomnia is defined as insomnia that lasts more than a month. It can be caused by an inability to fall asleep - also known as onset insomnia, or waking on and off during the night - also known as middle insomnia.

Symptoms include not being able to get back asleep after waking up too early or poor sleep quality.

Insomnia is one of the most prevalent mental health conditions, affecting up to 30% of individuals. Even if it occurs as part of another condition, it may still require special treatment (e.g., depression, generalized anxiety disorder, post-traumatic stress disorder).

As we discussed in the previous module, insomnia can be caused by a variety of factors, including stress or discomfort. Different things, on the other hand, keep the problem continuing most of the time. Sleep issues may be perpetuated by those who have negative ideas about sleep.

There are several forms of bad sleep thoughts.

1) When people don't get enough sleep, they can do one of two things: "I haven't slept well this week, thus I must not be able to sleep," as opposed to "I haven't slept well this week because I could be stressed at work or home, and I should deal with it."

2) Another prevalent style of thinking is to blame everything on a lack of sleep. People who don't get enough sleep may experience issues with their moods, focus, and memory. But sleep isn't the primary source of these issues. Insomniacs frequently believe their sleep troubles are to blame for everything that goes wrong throughout the day, but this is not the case.

3) People who have unreasonable assumptions about how much sleep they require might make sleeping problems much worse. Individuals who don't get enough sleep, for example, believe everyone requires eight hours of sleep every night to function well. When it comes to how much sleep a person needs, everyone is different. Some people require only four to five hours of sleep every night, while others require nine to ten. Setting severe restrictions or limits on how much sleep you should get will make you more anxious and falling asleep more difficult.

4) Catastrophizing, black-and-white thinking, overgeneralization, and making broad generalizations are all negative thinking patterns.

Sleep issues can also be exacerbated by selective attention. You may recall the periods when you slept poorly but not how well you slept. When you're trying to fall asleep, you should also pay attention to all your bodily reactions. As a result, insomniacs tend to categorize a night's sleep as either excellent or horrible, leaving little place for "good enough," "not bad at all," or "fine."

Let's consider sleep hygiene. This refers to how you treat your body before going to bed.

The term "sleep hygiene" is used to describe appropriate sleeping habits. A great deal of study has gone into developing a set of recommendations and advice to assist individuals in getting a good night's sleep. There is evidence that these techniques can help people obtain a decent night's sleep for a long period.

Insomnia is treated with a variety of medications, but most of them only work for a limited period. Long-term use of sleep medication can lead to addiction, making it more difficult to develop appropriate sleep patterns that aren't reliant on the pills. This could worsen your sleep issues. Your doctor can advise you on the best course of action. However, we believe proper sleep hygiene is an important aspect of managing insomnia. Other techniques, including medicine or cognitive therapy, can be used in addition to excellent sleep hygiene.

Suggestions for a restful night's sleep

1) Make sure you're on top of your game. Going to bed and getting up at the same time every day, including on weekends and days off, is a great method to teach your body to obtain a

good night's sleep. This will help you feel better and provide something for your body to do.

2) Get some rest when you're exhausted. Only try to sleep when you're weary or drowsy. Don't spend too much time in bed.

3) Get up and try once more. If you haven't fallen asleep in 20 minutes or more, get out of bed and do something calming or dull until you're ready to return to bed. Then, return to your bed and try again. Sit on the couch and peruse the phone book with the lights off. Your brain will be notified by the bright light that it is time to wake up. Don't do something too thrilling or engaging because this will make you more awake.

4) This is the fourth and last step you should take. Do not consume coffee or smoke cigarettes for at least four hours before going to bed. This is because these items can make you less tired. These drugs are stimulants, making it difficult to fall asleep.

5) There are five reasons why you should not use alcohol: It's also a good idea to avoid alcohol for at least four to six hours before going to bed. Many people believe that drinking alcohol relaxes them and helps them go to sleep. However, it prevents them from obtaining a good night's sleep and makes them weary.

6) Your bed should only be used for two things: sleep and to have sex. As a result, your body will begin to link your

bed with sleep rather than other activities. Your body will not learn this if you use your bed to read, work on your laptop, or pay bills.

7) Check if you're sleepy enough to go to bed. If you can't go an entire day without a nap, it's fine to take one. But make sure it's under an hour and before 3 pm!

8) You can notify your body it's time to sleep in a variety of ways. You can spend 15 minutes each night doing calming stretches or breathing exercises or sit quietly with a cup of caffeine-free tea.

9) It's bath time. Bathing in a hot tub can help you fall asleep because it raises your body temperature, which makes you sleepy as it decreases. When you're fatigued, your body temperature drops, making you drowsy.

10) Don't pay attention to the time. Many people who have problems sleeping keep an excessive watch on the clock. Checking the clock frequently in the middle of the night can cause you to wake up, especially if you use the light to see the time. This can lead to thoughts such as, "Oh no, look how late it is; I'll never get to sleep," or "It's so early, I've only slept for five hours; this is dreadful."

11) Use a sleep journal to keep track of your sleep. If you want to make sure you have the correct information regarding how well you sleep, this worksheet might help. You should

just keep a diary for two weeks to get a sense of what's going on and then revisit it two months later to assess how you've progressed. This is because keeping a journal necessitates checking the time (see point 10).

12) Get some exercise. You should exercise every day to help you sleep better. But don't overdo it in the four hours leading up to bedtime. A morning stroll is a terrific way to feel good as the day begins.

13) Eat healthily. This will help you sleep better, but you must eat at the appropriate times. A modest snack before bedtime might be beneficial, but a large meal immediately before bedtime can make it difficult to sleep. Some individuals believe that drinking a warm glass of milk, which contains tryptophan, will aid sleep. Tryptophan is a sleep aid that comes from nature.

14) The ideal location. It is important to have a peaceful bed and sleeping area in order to have a decent night's sleep. If there is noise outside your room, use earplugs, and make sure you have drapes or an eye mask to block out the early morning light. It's ideal to be in a chilly environment with plenty of blankets to keep you warm.

Ensure that your daytime routines do not change. Even if you've had a horrible night's sleep and are weary, keep your daytime activities the same. Even if you're exhausted, keep going. This may alleviate sleeplessness.

Dream interpretations.

There may be moments in our dreams when we wake up from a nightmare in which we are in a hazardous or life-threatening scenario, or we have made a mistake or been humiliated in front of others. Many things happen in these nightmares that appear to be extremely genuine, making them frightening or making you feel horrible. After we wake up, the sensations may linger for a few minutes or hours. It may be difficult to fall asleep again, or we may be plagued by them during the day. Our brains are only in a dream state for a few seconds at a time, according to brain scans. Even so, some nightmares appear to linger for a long period, yet this is not the case.

About 6% of individuals report they experience nightmares at least once a month, and 1% to 2% claim they have them on a regular basis. A person may experience several dreams with the same topic or various dreams with the same theme (e.g., loss of control).

Nightmare Disorder occurs when dreams occur frequently, cause significant discomfort, or have a detrimental impact on everyday life (e.g., inability to focus at work or school, depression, or anxiety). Having troubling dreams is one of the symptoms of Post-Traumatic Stress Disorder (PTSD). Without a direct relationship to prior traumatic experiences, frequent nightmares may happen on their own. Dreams can occur for a variety of causes, and some medications might increase the likelihood of their occurrence. It may be beneficial to speak with a medical expert about your nightmares.

What causes dreams to keep going?

Dreams can be very emotional for some individuals, yet they may not affect them. Others, on the other hand, are troubled by unpleasant dreams and experience difficulties in their well-being or everyday life as a result. It's not necessarily what we dream about but rather how we respond to them. Some of the things we may think about our dreams are "I'm weak and defenseless," "The world is scary," and "I can't deal with them." We could also believe that the dreams are out of our control, as in "I can't cope with them." Many individuals see these dreams as significant or powerful in some manner. "My dreams are attempting to tell me something essential," or "It's a warning that something horrible may happen." Many people feel that experiencing nightmares is unpleasant, and, as a result, they may worry about them more than they should. They may take steps to prevent them from occurring (e.g., avoid sleep, cut down daytime activities to save energy, distract themselves, etc.). These measures may assist for a short time, but they can also make you feel worse, and seldom halt or lessen nightmares.

These interpretations aren't very useful, whether you think your dreams are telling you you're weak and vulnerable or trying to tell you something significant.

We pay greater attention to our dreams when we think about them this way, which causes us to stress and overthink them.

To avoid or end nightmares, alter your behavior (e.g., avoid sleep, excessive daytime worries, substance use, limit daytime activities, etc.)

What options do I have for dealing with my nightmares?

_____

_____

_____

_____

_____

CBT (cognitive behavioral therapy) has been demonstrated to be an effective treatment for nightmares. CBT for nightmares aims to assist patients in identifying and changing some of the negative interpretations that are associated with their dreams, thus alleviating some of the anguish these nightmares bring. It also aims to identify and improve behaviors that may be contributing to nightmares, as well as provide us with more useful knowledge and habits about how we sleep and cope with nightmares.

Rewriting your pictures or practicing seeing them is another approach to dealing with nightmares. The first step is to decide which nightmares we want to focus on and mentally go over them. It's then up to us to rewind the vision and adjust it as we want in order to change some of the negative connotations and interpretations associated with our dreams. Because it might be frightening at first, many people begin this process with the help of a therapist. Image rescripting can be a useful tool for regaining control of our nightmares and increasing our confidence in dealing with them when they occur.

Imaging Rescripting is a treatment approach that helps people cope with disturbing or critical ideas in their brains that are keeping their mental health problems from getting better. Images from the past, nightmares, and future dreams are all common sources of distress for people.

Unpleasant recollections

If we've had a horrible experience in the past, it's common for the memory of that incident to haunt us. What we expect to happen today will be colored and tainted by it. It's difficult to let go of these memories, and we might become extremely engrossed in them.

When we've had a disturbing encounter, something happens. Because our minds struggle to understand what happened, we keep thinking about it. in this way, the memory is preserved. It never becomes a negative experience that belongs in the past. We strive to forget about the experience with every recollection and attempt to push the unpleasant memories away. But our thoughts may continuously bring up memories in order to keep us on high alert and prevent the negative occurrence from happening again.

Nightmares

Many people have recurring nightmares or dreams that make them feel awful. Dreams that repeat themselves could be the same or different, but they all have the same negative element. When individuals wake up after a nightmare, they frequently want to forget about it. They may find it difficult to fall asleep again, or they may begin to avoid sleeping because they don't want to have the dream repeated.

Future scenarios that are upsetting

We may think about something in great detail if we are worried or dreading something that may happen in the future. We may picture ourselves unable to cope, things going wrong, others disliking us, horrible things occurring to us or someone we care about, or other negative events. It'll happen again. We'll attempt to switch off the negative image running through our heads once we recognize it's there.

Using Images to Rescript

When someone encounters an unpleasant vision, a frequent reaction is to try to push the image away or erase it from their memory. This is what the majority of people do. We tend to be terrified of these pictures when we don't see them, making us much more afraid of the vision itself. This increases our fear of the image and gives it more power over us, elevating it above the status of "simply an image."

We employ imagery rescripting to work on these photographs. These photos are no longer avoided. Instead, we are making a concerted effort to visit them. That is, we close our eyes and mentally run through the visual. Then, we reverse the image and modify it the way we want. We change the story. Many people express a desire to be in command of their image on their own terms. Some rewrites may be more realistic now, while others will be pure imagination. When it comes to Imagery Rescripting, is there a limit to how much you can change the picture? In this sense, it may be very strong and innovative. It's conceivable that you'll edit the image in one direction and then change your mind. You may just replay the video and try something different to see how it fits.

Sometimes, you'll just consider how you'd like the picture to be different, what you'd do to make it less dangerous or safe, or what you require in an image and consider how you may alter the tale to fulfill that requirement.

You might enter the picture as your older, more compassionate self and do whatever you want to help and support your younger self. If the memory is from your younger years and is about something that happened, this could happen. If it proves too difficult at first, your therapist may step in and assist your younger self in any way that seems safe to them.

BONUS CHAPTER

MINDFULNESS & MEDITATION

Mindfulness is not just a therapy – it has been shown in research to create actual changes in the brain. Brain imaging performed on patients who have undergone mindfulness for anxiety and depression has led to the observation that the therapy alters the structures found in the brain, such as the reduction of cortical thinning, which is often associated with dementia and other age-related conditions. People who utilize mindfulness-based cognitive therapy are also able to enjoy more empathic awareness and higher emotional intelligence, which leads to more effective regulation of emotional abilities when compared to those who do not.

Walking with mindfulness

Walking meditation gives you a sense of grounding and allows you to let go of tension and worry. When you walk, you're usually going from one place to another, always moving to go someplace. Walking mindfully has a specific goal in mind; with each stride, you are bringing yourself closer to the present moment.

We all learned to walk as toddlers and have probably done it without thinking every day since. We take our feet's capacity to balance our bodies for granted.

Walking mindfully helps you become more aware of your body. As you go through the movements of walking, you begin to notice the movement of each foot. With each step, you raise the foot, push the foot ahead, and then lower the foot. This is a straightforward procedure, but you should complete one step before moving on to the next. "Lift your foot, move your foot, and position your foot." "Lift your foot, move your foot, and put your foot down." Slowly begin this process and become conscious of your body's movement. Throughout the day, there will be several modifications. Depending on the conditions, you'll walk slowly sometimes and swiftly at other times. Concentrate on the sensation of elevating each foot, pushing it forward, and then lowering it. Walking meditation can be done for a few minutes throughout the day.

1. Find a quiet area where you can walk back and forth for about 10 minutes without being interrupted, no more than 10 to 20 feet. Give this practice your whole attention.

- *Begin walking gently, observing the sensation on the bottoms of your feet as each foot contacts the ground, from the tips of your toes to the back of your heel. Pay attention to your complete body's movement when walking, not just your feet - the side-to-side motions of your hips, the back-and-forth swing of your arms.*
- *Take a breath and stand motionless for a moment. Take note of how your body feels when it stands on the ground.*
- *Listen to the noises, see the sights, and smell the aromas around you. Recognize whatever feelings or thoughts you have.*
- *Now start walking again, concentrating solely on walking as you shift your weight to the right leg and raise your left foot, pushing it forward and lowering it to the ground.*
- *Now move your weight to your left leg and raise your right foot off the ground, pushing it forward and back down.*
- *Slowly resume walking. Notice the sensation on the bottoms of your feet as each foot contacts the ground, from the tips of your toes to the back of your heel. Pay attention to your hips' side-to-side motions and your arms' back-and-forth swings.*
- *Pay attention to each step until you reach your specified stop point. Then, focus on the intricate process of turning and walking back to your starting location with concentration.*
- *Concentrate fully on each step.*
- *Repeat the process, walking, turning, and returning to your starting location one step at a time.*
- *Take a mindful walk.*

2. Measure roughly twenty paces of level ground (or a clearly defined walk between two trees) as your meditation path if you have access to a garden, some open area, or even a hallway. Change the length of the walkway to fit what's available in tighter spaces.

- *Stand at one end of the route and concentrate on your body's feelings. Allow your focus to be drawn to the sensation of your body standing erect, arms naturally positioned, and hands softly clasped in front or behind you or hanging by your sides. Allow your eyes to stare at a point around three meters [10 feet] in front of you at ground level, keeping your neck in alignment with your spine. Maintain gentle attention while remaining motionless.*

- *Investigate how the body moves. The hips and lower back are where the movement starts. Walk forward from your hips, elevating each leg slightly as you swing it forward. Allow your hips to turn slightly with each step. It's worth noting that the hips' movement is synchronized with a tiny bend in the shoulders. When one leg swings forward, the accompanying shoulder turns backward to compensate. Don't overdo this movement; instead, see it as an indication that the body is walking as one unit, rather than as a head going forward with a body underneath it. Allow the world to come to you rather than thrusting yourself into it.*

- *To get to the end of the trail, take it slowly and deliberately. Stop. For a few breaths, concentrate on the body standing.*

Bring up the mindset of beginning over, then turn around and walk back.

- *Be aware of the broad flow of bodily sensations while walking, or focus your attention more intently on your feet. Return your focus to the sensations of your feet contacting the ground, the intervals between each stride, and the sensations of halting and beginning.*

- *Adapt your tempo to your mood: brisk when drowsy or preoccupied with thoughts, firm and steady when restless and impatient. Keep your pace constant and allow things to move through your consciousness as you walk to bring energy and fluidity to the practice. Rather than getting engrossed with the issue, consider the stream of ideas, perceptions, and feelings as a flow. When your mind becomes absorbed, your focus becomes fixed on a topic, and you begin to add a lot more information and story. Also, note your thoughts and where they lead you – into the past or future, toward self-doubt or other people. Consider: how much of this rambling thinking is beneficial or relevant to our health. Is it okay to put these topics aside for a few moments? Then attempt to refocus your attention on your body walking. Every moment, start over. This provides a sense of regeneration, which helps to keep the mind fresh.*

3. Let's do some more walking.

- *Begin with one of your feet. Pick it up, move it across space, and set it softly on the ground, sensing the sensations of each step from heel to toe. Taking up a foot, making a decision,*

> picking up a foot, lifting it, moving it through space, feeling it touch down from heel to toe.

- Walk with purpose. We're so used to walking on "automatic pilot," where we're essentially tuned out and just letting the body flow. You might realize that being so deliberate about walking feels a little weird. That's OK. This goal is a means for you to reconnect with the current moment and how you're feeling right now.

- Pay attention to yourself. Take in as much as you can about the sensations of lifting up your foot, moving it through space, and then gently putting it down. I understand that most of us are so used to walking that when we first notice it, we may feel a bit unsteady. It's fine: this is natural, and it's part of what it's like to wake up and pay attention to the specifics of our activities.

- Pay attention to the task at hand. Right now, concentrate on the sensation of your feet making contact with the earth. Is there a difference between thinking about your feet and really experiencing them touching the ground or the floor? Can you allow yourself to feel grounded and connected as you make the intentional decision to be there for this walk?

- Pay attention to your surroundings. Allow yourself to feel the impact of the air on your skin if you choose to step outside. What do you think you've noticed? Is it hot or cold? Is the air humidified or dry? Allow yourself to be affected by it.

- Pay attention to when your ideas take over. You could notice how fast your attention is pulled to your thoughts, whether they're daydreaming, writing a list, or replaying an old *conversation or narrative in your head. You may realize that being lost in contemplation makes it more difficult to connect with your senses after you recognize your thoughts trying to hijack your stroll. You'll probably find it's tougher to hear what's going on around you and smell and taste things. That is the power of thought. So, when you realize your thoughts are drawing you away, simply acknowledge it, smile, and then gently and lovingly choose to turn your attention to your felt sensations and especially back to the sensation of your feet walking. Throughout your stroll, bring your attention back to this sensory and physical experience.*

Connect to the Here and Now.

- *Allow yourself to be aware of your surroundings. What do you think of the weather right now? Do you have any thoughts on the subject? What if you just notice that the weather is present, recognizing its attributes and how you're experiencing it on your skin or in your body? What happens if you allow yourself to be aware of the sounds that surround you? What do the odors surrounding you make you notice? Can you imagine these sensory characteristics as the world's symphony?*

The world's smells are strong, acidic, sweet, sour, fresh, and earthy. You may hear high-pitched and low-pitched hums that are loud or faint. How much can you allow yourself to take in the environment as your senses experience it without adding a layer of judgment about how you feel? For the time being, see what you can accomplish while you absorb the raw facts of the environment around you during your morning stroll.

- *Take a breather now and again. Another method to enhance the sensory experience of this walk is to stop in your tracks now and then if you're able and it's acceptable. Note how it feels to be grounded when your feet touch the soil or the floor in a very precise way. Take time to choose something specific to see with your eyes, focusing on color, form, and texture.*

  Allow your nose to take in a deep breath and smell the air. Redirect your focus to your ears and listen to the world as it is right now. Can you carry whatever you're seeing lightly and allow it to be a part of your surroundings as you experience it? You don't have to judge it, modify it, or intervene in any way. Just be here for you right now, and when you're ready, choose which foot you'll start walking with and resume your stroll.

  9. Set your own pace. As you walk, pay attention to which foot is moving as you lift it up, move it through space, and softly set it down, feeling the foot make contact with the ground. Although traveling slowly at first may be beneficial, once you've learned to be present while walking in this new style, there's no reason you can't go faster. Find a speed that allows you to be present while experiencing.

  Be inquisitive and allow your mind to wander.

- *Experiment with aimless roaming. You might utilize this early wake-up stroll to get to work or any other specific location. Allowing oneself to go for an aimless walk might be fantastic provided you feel secure doing so. Setting a timer for 15 minutes and letting your feet lead you wherever they want to go, keeping present in your ever-changing environment without having a goal as a destination, could be a good idea. As you heighten your senses with this early stroll, notice how it feels to reconnect to inner impulses that come up as everything begins to calm a little. Observing how the attention is pulled to other things, notably thinking, over and over.*

Bringing your focus back to your feet again and over again can be the most effective way to reconnect with the present moment, as you let your felt senses and the sensation of your feet contacting the ground draw you back, right now, over and over. Take note of how you feel after your stroll and check in with each of your senses. What are you aware of now that you've spent this time focusing on your sensory experiences? What changes have you seen in your mood recently? Take note of how it feels to be in your body and aware of your precious existence.

A Meditation for Loss and Grief

1. First, choose a comfy place and relax. Slowly inhale and exhale deeply. Relax and settle in, allowing yourself to be fully immersed in the present moment. What exactly is going on in your life right now?

2. Now consider a personal loss. It might be the recent death of a friend, relative, or loved one; it could also be a loss you've been carrying for a long time as a weight. It's not something you've read about or anything distant or abstract, but rather something intimate, like a person, an event, or a part of your life.

3. Begin with your body and the physical sensation you're having right now. What physical sensations do you have? Do you have a sense of being rooted? Or are you edgy, dull, squirmy, tight, hollow, or full? What do you think you've noticed? Don't try to make sense of it; just experience it. Right now, what is your body trying to tell you?

4. Now, turn your attention to your heart in the center of your chest. Imagine your heart carrying the sadness and being filled and weighed down by it. Your beating heart is raw, gentle, loving, and vulnerable. And then you may relax.

5. Now relax in the middle of your throat. Grief is often associated with the throat. And it has a tightness and soreness to it that we get when we're going to cry, when we're surprised, or when we're grieving. Look for other places in your body where your sadness is held. It might be your heart, throat, or stomach. They're all holding something, digesting something—and the body understands it without words or guidance.

6. Next, pay attention to the feelings that are manifesting. Sorrow, fury, a quality of love, disappointment, and a sensation of intensity or dullness might all be present. Take note of the feelings that arise. Don't be embarrassed or scared to express yourself. Don't pass judgment on how you're feeling. Just go with your gut. Allow your feelings to surface. Welcome them warmly. Don't suffocate them, and don't feed them either. Our grief's energy is expressed via our emotions. They also change. They're ever-changing, just like life. Be kind to yourself. Take a moment, rest, and breathe if you start to feel overwhelmed. Resettle. Allow yourself to relax and enjoy your current bodily emotional state.

7. Simply relax, experience, and be. Allow grief to do its thing. Allow it to cure you. Don't be too pushy. Don't be irritable. Allow yourself to be sad. Consider how you're going to deal with this shift in your life. Allow it to instruct you.

8. Consider your own sadness, the losses you've experienced, and how your losses link you to so many others. Just bringing that reality to your attention could be helpful. It can happen to anyone. Change is difficult to accept. It's difficult to say goodbye. However, when you stop battling the inevitability of loss and change, you might experience a new and deeper love and respect. We don't take our friends, our loved ones, or our lives for granted any longer. Through this painful road, through loss, sadness, and sorrow, with an open and soft heart, we release our love, joy, and appreciation in a very powerful way.

Arrive, Breathe, Connect: A 12-Minute Meditation

1. Get into a position that is vigilant yet relaxed for you. You may need to change your posture somewhat to get comfortable in your chair. Place your feet flat on the floor, your bottom in the seat of your chair, and then sit up straight. You may relax your hands by laying them on top of your thighs, palms down. Then, if you're comfortable, carefully lower your gaze or close your eyes.

2. Pause for a second to thoroughly immerse yourself in the current moment. Are you at work or doing something else? Of course, if you're driving, it's probably a good idea to pull over for a while. In any event, give yourself the gift of a moment of attention and clarity by taking this opportunity to be present. Allow yourself to let go of your to-do list. Allow whatever comes next to pass. You're making a firm commitment to be present in this moment.

3. Run your hand over your body, checking in and experiencing the temperature. You may also consider if you're feeling particularly grounded, ungrounded, or buried right now. You don't have to do anything about it, just be aware.

4. Now turn your focus inside to your own breathing. Notice inhalations and exhalations wherever they feel most apparent. You'll feel the most at the tip of your nose, where chilly air enters the nostrils. And at your mouth as you exhale the warm breath. Alternatively, you may experience a full breath, going from your nose through your throat, chest, and belly.

5. Make a connection with a few bodily experiences. Notice the ones we can link to the energy we wish to work with when we show up with guts and dignity. In your mind's eye, start tracing your spine from the tailbone to the lower back, upper back, back of the neck, and crown of the head. Feel the length of your spine while doing so. You can even feel as if you're expanding a little, with greater space between your vertebrae and spine.

Allow your head to rest comfortably on your spine.

6. As you feel the length of your spine, notice how it gives you a sense of dignity and a grounded and balanced stance. Then, imagine your back. Feel how wide it is. Take note of the distance between one shoulder and the next, as well as the distance between one underarm and the other. To access this location, you can even breathe more deeply into the back of the rib cage. Feel into your strength with your breadth. This part of the body is associated with strength, grit, focus, and resolve.

7. Now turn your focus to the front of your chest, where the breastbone is. Initially, your mind's eye may only perceive a small region. Try to concentrate on the space around that point, taking in the entire chest. Feel your heart pumping under your breastbone and your warmth. Consider the spirit that is peaceful, compassionate, and welcoming. And that's what we'll refer to as your grace.

8. Notice the length of your spine and the sense of dignity once more. Notice of the length of your back, your strength, and your determination. Take note of the warmth in your chest, your heart, and your humanity. Allow these three sensations to interact: dignity, grit, and strength.

9. Take a few deep breaths in and out. Bring your fingers and toes back to life with a few little motions. Open your eyes if they've been closed. You can begin to lift your focus if your eyes have been downcast.

Welcome Everything with a 12-Minute Meditation

To welcome something does not imply we must like or agree with it. It just means that we must be open to meeting it. We put our rush to judge on hold for the moment and simply observe what's going on.

With the ability to welcome comes the ability to deal with what is there, whether good or bad.

1. Sit back in your chair, relax, and focus on your breath and body. If it's more comfortable for you, try closing your eyes. Allow your breathing to be as natural as possible.

2. Start by becoming aware of your body's varied sensations: pressure, movement, tingling, and the sensation of air on your hands and face. Just let the waves of feeling wash over you.

3. Let go of the concept of limbs, legs, and a body now. Recognize the space above your head. What is the size of that space? Allow your awareness to pick up on what's to your left. What's over there to your right? Allow your consciousness to descend into the space underneath your body. Is there any movement in your feet or on the ground? Allow your consciousness to expand to the area behind your body so that it encompasses the entire space. Allow your consciousness to be aware of what's in front of the body, spreading out as far as it possibly can, creating a sensation of openness, of vast space, in which all of the actions of the body, heart, and mind emerge and disappear.

4. Allow all experiences to occur naturally, with no intervention from the inside or outside. Relax your control over your thoughts. Examine the distinction between being lost in thought and being aware of it. When a sound in the room happens or a bird passes by, you just observe the sound of the bird and do not believe it is you. Allow your thoughts and feelings to flow in this manner, everything arriving and departing in a large, open area. Consider what occurs when you go into a room. Most people focus on the chairs, tables, and other things in the room and fail to see the space.

5. Allow yourself to be aware of the area where all the activity, all the coming and going, takes place. Remember that everything we can provide room for can move. Allow all ideas, sensations, and feelings to rise and fall in the broad expanse like clouds in the sky.

6. Finally, bring your focus to awareness itself. It is open, transparent, and clear, unaffected by anything that comes and goes. Nothing should be pushed away; everything should be welcomed.

Relaxation Meditation Script of 15 Minutes

1: Create a soothing environment

It is, of course, beneficial to meditate in a calm environment if you wish to employ meditation for relaxation. This is where my guide on establishing a Zen room comes in.

Essentially, you want to make sure that your space is peaceful and relaxing. Make sure your area is free of obstructions. You may always play soothing music in the background, such as birdsong or Tibetan Singing Bowls, if that helps. Distract yourself as much as possible. Also, ensure that the room is properly aired, ideally with fresh air. Sunlight can also assist because it has a calming effect on us.

2: Maintain a decent posture while sitting.

Before you begin meditating, make sure you are sitting or lying in a posture that allows your body to relax. Remember that meditation isn't only for the mind; it's also for the body, and your body must be quiet, tension-free, and relaxed. Before you begin meditating, you might find it helpful to do a few mindful stretches. As a result, your body will be ready.

3: Start by focusing on your breath.

We'll practice Anapanasati meditation.

Begin by concentrating on the movement of your breath between your lips. You should be able to hear your breath if your mind is quiet enough.

Begin to notice how your breath moves throughout your body after around twenty breaths. Your mind will begin to calm, and you will feel a sense of inner serenity and relaxation. Consider how you feel.

4: We're going to undertake a self-guided relaxation meditation now.

We'll concentrate on a soothing sight. Personally, I enjoy daydreaming about being in a forest or by the water.

Assume you're sitting in a forest on the grass, near the sea. The towering trees are seen rising above you. All around you are the sounds of birds chirping in the woods. You can see the waves of the sea lapping on the coast in front of you, and you hear the swooshing of the water. Take your time to imagine these things thoroughly.

When we envision things like this, we quiet the mind, which is one of the benefits of meditation for relaxation. Such sights are calming and might assist in alleviating any tension you may be feeling. So, take a moment to picture that situation in your mind's eye.

5: Recite the Om mantra

Melt away with the mantra Om (pronounced "Aum") in the second level of our 15-minute meditation script for relaxation.

Om is a primal sound and the most holy mantra in Hindu and Buddhist theology, expressing ultimate truth. Another advantage of meditation for relaxation is that it causes mild reverberations around the body that assist in relaxing the muscles and organs.

Begin by uttering the sound Om. Take note of how wide and round the sound is. It reverberates in your tongue and throughout your body, softly caressing you and assisting you in relaxing.

Allow your entire body to relax and remove any tension while you focus on the sound "Om." Instead, rather than trying to control this mantra, let it travel where it will. Attempt to immerse your conscious awareness in the mantra so that your mind merges with it.

Because 108 is an auspicious number typically used, I prefer to recite Aum 108 times (mantra recitation).

You should find your mind and body sinking further into the music with each Aum until the sound is all you are experiencing. You will have perfect inner serenity at this moment. Your thoughts will be muted for the time being (which is the main benefit of meditation for relaxation).

6: Completed

Our relaxing meditation script is now complete. However, if you want to feel comfortable after you meditate, make sure you finish correctly.

Don't just open your eyes and continue with your business. Instead, gradually and slowly open your eyes, repeating to yourself, "Opening... opening..." Carry the sensation of inner serenity and relaxation with you while you accomplish this.

Close your eyes again, breathe a few more times, and then gently open your eyes again if you find yourself losing your inner serenity. When you first open your eyes, you must feel comfortable and in a meditative condition.

Meditation script for deep serenity with essential oils

1. Pick a smell that relaxes you, such as lavender. Light a candle with that aroma or make your own scent in whatever way you desire (you can simply meditate on lavender soap if you like)

2. Close your eyes and take ten slow, deep breaths in and out through your nostrils.

3. Become aware of the soothing aroma.

4. Concentrate on the soothing aroma and become one with it.

5. If ideas arise, consciously notice them and let them go.

6. Take 100 breaths while concentrating on the fragrance.

Managing negative emotions

When you're having a bad day, do the following:

1. Stop.

2. Keep in mind that a sensation is simply that: an emotion.

3. Allow the emotion to be what it is. There's nothing else.

4. Pay attention to how you're feeling.

"This is only a sensation," you may say.

6. Accept it as it is.

7. Don't let it grow into something bigger.

Inner tranquility meditation script.

1. Close your eyes for a moment.

2. Tell yourself, "I'm getting calmer and more relaxed."

3. Take ten deep breaths through your nose while focusing on the movement of the breath.

4. Recite the Om mantra.

5. Pay attention to how the mantra makes you feel in your body. It's cozy and soothing.

6. Take a deep breath and continue to focus on "Om" for another 100 breaths.

Meditation in the Forest for Inner Peace

1. Take a seat in your garden.

2. Close your eyes and begin to feel the garden's feelings. The smells, the sounds, and the emotions.

3. Notice how the world supports your body by feeling the grass embracing you.

4. Feel the breeze on your face. Is it hot or chilly outside? Consider that feeling for a moment.

5. Now open your eyes and notice the different shades of flowers and grass.

6. Listen to the sounds of birds, water, or other soothing sounds in the environment.

7. Show your appreciation for your garden. Remind yourself that you may come back here at any moment to unwind.

Anxiety Mindfulness Meditation Guided Script

You might also want to try these anxiety-relieving meditations.

1: [1 minute] Maintain appropriate posture while sitting or standing so you feel secure.

When meditating, correct posture is usually vital, but it's crucial when practicing an anxiety-meditation script.

With your feet shoulder-width apart, sit or stand with a straight spine (with a natural curvature at the bottom).

You'll be able to tell whether you have good posture since you'll feel more stable and stronger.

In an anxiety meditation script, posture is crucial for a reason. Proper posture causes your breathing to calm down, and produces GABA neurotransmitters, which lessen anxiety symptoms.

Having proper posture can help you relax and focus whether you meditate sitting or standing.

2: [5 minutes] Begin by breathing in squares. Inhale for four breaths. Hold for four seconds. Exhale for four counts. Hold for four minutes.

Take a four-second inhale. Hold the position for four seconds. Take a four-second exhale. Hold the position for four seconds. Repeat.

3: [5 minutes] While breathing, focus on the movement of your breath around your body.

You're starting to feel calmer, although your mind may still be racing with ideas.

It's now time to deal with those bothersome ideas. To do so, we'll spend five minutes practicing mindful breathing.

Focus on the space between your upper lip and your nose as you continue to Box Breathe. Allow your consciousness to settle in that place. Pay attention to the feeling of your breath as it moves through the area. Keep your attention here for a few minutes.

Now, shift your attention to the motion of your breath as it travels from your nose to your pelvis. For a few minutes, concentrate on this.

Observe and calmly classify your ideas as they come in.

You should be feeling more comfortable by now, and most of your anxious sensations should have subsided. However, you may discover you are having thoughts and anxieties, and that your mind gets caught up in them, interfering with your meditation.

Continue to concentrate on the movement of your breath through your body.

Now start labeling what's going on in your head. If you have a notion, tell yourself, "This is only a thought." "This is only a feeling," you might remark if you're having a bad day. Say "Mind becoming lost" when your mind gets lost in your thoughts for a time, then "Mind returning" when it returns.

This increases our awareness of mental movements and mental events. As a result, we become less receptive to various mental states. This is a modified version of Buddhist Vipassana meditation.

If you can't seem to quit overthinking, try this overthinking meditation script.

[10 minutes] 5: Slowly and deliberately travel your consciousness down your body, from the head to the toes, monitoring feelings and requesting each area of your body to relax.

We've now calmed down, lowered worry, and raised our level of awareness. Everything is making us feel a lot better.

Then there's dealing with bodily feelings.

Anxiety and bodily feelings are inextricably linked. Physical signs of anxiety, include a racing heart and shortness of breath. The mind can sometimes misinterpret physical sensations as indicating something is wrong.

For example, I occasionally have a quivering feeling in my chest. When I observe this, I get the feeling that something is very wrong. However, it's only a fleeting bodily sense.

We must learn to react emotionally to physical stimuli rather than reacting emotionally to them. In order to accomplish this, we conduct a Body Scan.

Moving your conscious awareness from the pinnacle of your head to your toes is what you want to do (the whole process should take approximately ten minutes).

While you're doing this, keep a calm eye on your body's sensations. Say to yourself, "This is simply a sensation" if any sensations make you feel uneasy. Then ask that particular area of your body to unwind.

Imagining breathing fresh air into tight portions of the body might assist.

6: [2 minutes] For a few minutes, sit, breathe, and relax.

Luminosity

Take a deep breath and allow the stress to leave your physical body as you exhale. Take a few slow, deep breaths. Mentally scan your entire body, noting how it feels. Concentrate your attention on the regions where tension is accumulated. Concentrate on the parts that feel constrained and begin to relax each one.

Feel your body become increasingly relaxed. The tension gradually dissipates. Stress is gradually being released. Slowly, I'm becoming more at peace. As you continue to let the breath flow, you may discover that you're relaxing more and more, and as you become more aware of the light within and around you, you'll get even more peaceful.

Make the mental image of a protective light glowing around your body. It's almost as though you're glistening. As the breath expands with each inhalation, the light expands as well. This light can keep you secure and present at this time in periods of stress, anxiety, and concern, and in any other situation where a brilliant light is required.

Start breathing into your light. Allow the light to continue to expand as you inhale, and as you exhale, allow the light to brighten. For the next few seconds, practice this. Allow the light to find its path — anchored, calm, and bright — as you inhale and expand into your light.

Imagine yourself surrounded by this light in your head. As the protective light surrounds you, you will feel a sense of relaxation, tranquility, and security. The light acts as a barrier. Anything that isn't useful at this time gets deflected. It's like light armor that protects, relaxes, calms, and secures you.

Imagine being engulfed in a protective glow that extends from the top of your head to the soles of your feet. When you take a deep breath, the light expands. The light brightens as you exhale.

Place your concentration on the core of your heart. Allow the light to make its way to the center of your heart. Invite a deep breath in as you envision this spark of light expanding into the protective light that surrounds your body. Return that energy to the heart place as you exhale. Inhale and extend your light into this protective barrier, then exhale and pull it back to your heart core. For the following several seconds, locate this practice. Your light will be illuminated and brightened.

Allow this light to spread and deepen as you continue to expand and deepen your breath, encompassing your entire physical area. Allow the light to increase into its protective shell on the inhale, and allow the light to brighten on the exhale. Begin to utilize light as a vehicle to expand into any regions in the body that seem dull, tight, or heavy. Expand the light when you take a deeper inhale. Allow the light to brighten as you exhale. As you breathe into the light, let your body continue to discover its area of alertness, relaxation, and calmness.

Allow yourself to return your consciousness and focus to the core of the heart as you continue to grow and explore your light. Begin to become aware of the area that surrounds the heart's core. Bring attention to the space that surrounds the body's protective shell. Allowing your light to radiate outward from your center. Feel the calmness spread out from the core of your body to your back, chest, hips, and legs. Feel the safety and tranquility that your body provides. You'll see that your body is encased in a luminous barrier.

Allow the relaxation to flow through your entire body, from the crown of your head to the soles of your feet. Feel each part of your body relax – peaceful, relaxed, and aware. Feel the protecting glow all around your body.

Protective light surrounds you from head to toe. Relax and bask in protecting light, shielded from any stress, strain, or concern.

As you progress through this technique, you may discover that some portions of your body are still tense. There may be some lingering diversions or anxieties in the mind. Allow oneself to be aware of these areas. Take note of the distraction. Allow yourself to drag out the concern, the distraction, with each breath by employing the protecting light. As they are physically released, feel the worry and tension leave the body, mind, and this moment. Continue to take deep breaths into the shielding light.

Continue to expand into the protecting barrier as you inhale, and bring that light in and allow it to intensify as you exhale. Allow the protecting light to draw tranquil ideas to you. It's like a magnet for awareness. A relaxing magnet. A focal point magnet. Attracting to you this current moment of silence, seclusion, and relaxation. Feel the protecting glow brighten, diverting attention away from you and offering tranquility. Allow it to insulate and protect you while also calming you down.

Continue to pay attention to your light. Continue to enhance your light with each breath. As you go from breath to breath, moment to instant, and into your light, continue to observe the feelings that come. If the mind wanders, observe what it is thinking about and return consciousness back to your light's embodiment and protective barrier. You're in a good mood. You appear to be at ease. You appear to be at ease. You appear to be at ease.

You are aware of the situation. You're in a good mood. You appear to be at ease. You appear to be at ease. You appear to be at ease.

Take note of the brightness of the light within you as well as the light that surrounds you. Become conscious of how safe and protected you feel as a result of your shield of protected light. Enjoy the sensation of being safe and secure behind your barrier of shielded light. It's time to return to work on the rest of your day. Remember that you may conjure up this protecting light whenever you need it. You may utilize your protecting light to relieve stress, anxiety, and worry and to feel calm, relaxed, and serene.

Return your attention to your breathing. Inhaling and exhaling deeply. Now concentrate on your body's reawakening. Gently move your body. It's a good feeling to be able to feel your muscles move. Allow your thoughts to become fully awake and attentive while contemplating and recording the sensation of calm. When you're ready, completely awake, fully energetic, totally peaceful, and fully relaxed, open your eyes.

Namaste.

A 20-Minute Meditation to Examine Interconnection

1. Sit, lay, or stand in a comfortable position. Simply be present in your body and breathe. I ask you to shut your eyes or lower your gaze till you see a crease of light.

2. Pay attention to what's coming up for you, what your body is sensing right now. How are you feeling right now? Take note of how your body breathes. There will be no judgment, only observation. From the inside out, check in with the interwoven unity we share with our bodies.

3. Take a deep inhale through your nose, all the way to the top of your lungs. Soften by letting go of the breath. Expel all of the air from your lungs until the bottom of the breath is reached. Observe how your body breathes. Remember who you are, what you stand for, and the linked self that lies under the surface of your existence. Allow yourself to relax and submit. Give in to your old self-concepts. Breathe. Take a deep breath. Also, keep in mind who you are.

4. Remember what's beneath you while you sit, recline, or stand: the layers of us. And give up the body. Breathe. Feel the ground under your feet supporting your body.

5. Become aware of your body and your breath. Your body is only a tool; you are not your body. You are the higher light and energy vibration. Take a deep breath and respect the tool.

6. Be grateful for the feet that support you. Take notice of your feet and the ground underneath them. Feet should be softer. Breathe. And then there's capitulation.

7. Gently massage the ankles and calves. Feel the ground's vibrations pulling your legs up and softening your knees and thighs. Feel the breath, remember who you are, and why we're all here: in unity with the body, mind, and higher vibrational self.

8. Relax your hips and buttocks. Give up your body. Allow the body to take a few deep breaths. Release the belly button and pay attention to your lower back and sacrum. There, take in the light and space.

9. Allow the breath to awaken your thoughts. Relax your stomach, seat, and intestines. Take note of the dualism of that body space. Take a deep breath. Soften. Remember who you are and how you are connected to your energy self. As the heart rises with profound love, feel the torso breathing with fullness. And then there's capitulation.

10. Make the spine softer. Back strain should be released. As the weight from the shoulders is released, your arms will become heavy. As the arms are drawn down, feel the neck lengthen.

11. Soften the fingers, which reflect the finer points of life. Let go of your hands' palms. What do you cling to in your life? Surrender, soften, and take a deep breath. As a tool, use the breath and the body.

12. Extend your wrists and forearms. Elbows, biceps, and triceps should all be softer. Breathe. Feel lightness in your arms, your embrace's tool. What do you cling to? Soften by taking a few deep breaths. Give up your body. Allow your thoughts to flow freely. Your physique is not who you are. The body serves as a tool. What are your plans for it?

13. Bring your attention to your neck. The throat should be relaxed and open. Tension in the jaw and mouth should be released. How do you communicate using your mouth? Soften the corners of your mouth. Respect the words that come from a place of intention and action. Face and jaw should be relaxed.

14. Bring your attention to your ears. Pay attention to and absorb everything you hear and see. Surrender. Observe how your body breathes. Bring your attention to your eyes. Eyelids and brows should be softened. Pay attention to what you're seeing. What you look at is remembered by your mind. It keeps track of what the eyes and ears see and hear. Do you see what I mean? Or do you avert your gaze? Relax and trust that your heart is listening.

15. Relax the mind and body by focusing on the breath. The breath is a tool that may assist us in softening our bodies and remembering who we are. The breath is a sign, a symbol of this connective movement. It is a pleasure to be able to breathe. The movement within us is sparked by our breathing. Give up your body. Feel your breath and utilize your skills to breathe into your higher-vibrational self.

16. Notice how the body is breathing, how it is linked, and how it is motionless. This is the start of a movement. Keep in mind who you are. Remember who you are underneath the surface and submit to your greater self. We are energy beings who are pulsating in unison, in light and are interconnected.

17. Take a deep breath. Inhale deeply through your nose and exhale slowly. Repeat this process two more times. Hold your breath for a moment. Hold for a few seconds before releasing. Keeping in mind what you stand for: our interconnectivity.

18. Bring your palms together and bring them to your heart. Inhale with gratitude for the luxury of breathing, for we all have the ability to do so. Exhale and bend your head to respect those who are unable to breathe.

A 20-Minute Meditation to Help You Fall Asleep

Recognize that there is nothing to push or make happen while considering any meditation linked to sleep. Set out to practice without any precise expectations or goals, as trying makes sleeping more difficult. We can't force ourselves to sleep, but by focusing on being calm and letting go of our thoughts, we may find ourselves dozing off.

There will be no ending bell or instruction for the meditation that follows. Finally, continue to practice if you want, or get a good night's sleep if you choose.

1. Begin by laying down and letting your legs rest in a comfortable hip-width apart position. You can rest your arms at your sides or lay your hands on your stomach.

2. Start by focusing on your breathing. Pay attention to the bodily movement associated with breathing, such as your belly rising and falling, as much as you can. Alternatively, you might concentrate your attention on the air passing in and out of your nose and mouth.

3. It's natural, even expected, to have a lot of ideas. Your mind rehashes the day's events or becomes preoccupied with concerns about the future. Recognize your bad behaviors and work on letting them go. Return to observing the breath after labelling whatever has caught your attention. Inhaling... and exhaling... and inhaling... and exhaling... and inhaling... and.

4. Check in with compassion for yourself if you get caught up in effort, irritation, or fear. Catch self-criticism or dissatisfaction in your thoughts and return to just one breath, one more time. Thoughts are just that: thoughts. Inhale... exhale... inhale... exhale... inhale... exhale. There isn't anything you need to correct or alter right now. Keep track of your ideas and mark them as "thoughts." Over and over, come back to one next breath.

5. *Pay attention to your body's sensations. Begin by focusing on the physical feelings in your feet. You don't have to wriggle your toes or move your feet; simply pay attention to them—the temperature, the pressure of your heel on the blanket or mat underneath you.*

6. *Move your focus from your feet down your lower legs, observing anything that catches your eye. Allow yourself to let go of notions of wanting to make anything happen. Then up through your knees and into your upper legs from your lower legs. If you're feeling stressed or tense, try to relax and let go.*

7. *Now shift your focus to your buttocks and pelvis, as well as your gut and abdomen. You could feel your breath flowing up and down, or other bodily sensations, or perhaps an emotional reflection (perhaps an emotion like fear or anger reflects in the stomach in the form of tension or tightness). And as you proceed from your belly button to your chest, take note of any times your mind wanders to unpleasant or distracting ideas. Then softly and patiently guiding it back for a third time.*

8. *Move to your back, which is a common source of stress for many of us. Relax your muscles as much as possible, dropping your shoulders from your ears. If you sense the desire to make a change, do it with intention, stopping before deciding your next step. Shift your focus to your hands and lower arms, observing and letting go without actively moving or changing anything.*

9. *Moving through your neck and into the muscles of your face, maybe recognizing any areas of tension or pinching, and then gently releasing those muscles as best you can. After that,*

experience a general awareness of physical feelings throughout your body for a few seconds.

10. Now, if you're still awake, return your focus to the breath whenever your mind goes into the past, future, or anywhere it decides to go. You can count breaths if it's a beneficial anchor for your attention: breathing in, one, breathing out, one, breathing in, two, breathing out, two... Restart at one when you reach ten.

11. If counting becomes a distraction, simply focus on the feeling of breathing—wherever you feel your abdomen and chest rising and falling as the breath enters or leaves your body. Continue counting breaths up to ten on your own now, gently restoring your focus anytime you feel distracted. It's alright if you lose track of the numbers. Restart at the point where you last remembered.

A 20-Minute Meditation on Loving-Kindness

1. Begin by paying attention to your body in this moment. Is there anything you could make different? Is there anything you can soften or encourage to soften? Do you relax your heart, chest, and belly?

2. Allow gravity to take control of your life. Allow yourself to submit and relax into the sensation of being supported. Feeling supported by the chair or the earth beneath your feet. Even the earth is on your side.

3. Put your hand against your body. You might place it on your chest, your heart, or another part of your body. As we continue with this technique, let your hands be a type of calming, gentle support.

4. Take a few deep breaths and wish yourself well, allowing yourself to experience the love and support that comes from merely touching your own hand. Wishing oneself well might be challenging, so try a few different approaches. You may think of all the traits you admire in yourself for a moment or imagine someone who truly loves you and recognizes your kindness. It might be a significant other, a close friend, or even a pet. Take advantage of this opportunity to reconnect with your own goodness.

5. Recite the phrases loving-kindness and self-compassion for a few moments. You can experiment with some of these phrases to find what works best for you. May I be content with myself as I am. May my body be robust and healthy. I totally adore myself.

6. While keeping connected to your physical body, repeat one word or phrase and imagine yourself soaking up these good wishes, bathing every inch of your body with happiness and relaxation.

7. You may begin to move your sentiments of love and gratitude to someone else when you're brimming with them. Consider a person in your life who makes it simple for you to adore them. I wish for them to be well, happy, and at ease.

8. As you finish your meditative practice, carry this feeling of loving-kindness and compassion with you into the world.

A 15-Minute Self-Acceptance Meditation

1. Get into a straight position. Close your eyes or cast a delicate look downward. Relax your arms at your sides and place your feet on the ground. Place your hands in your lap and relax. Draw your shoulder blades inwards slightly, enabling your chin to be parallel to the floor. Raise your brows to the heavens and lift the crown of your head. Soften the belly button and the jaw.

2. Notice how it feels to come to a complete halt. Consider how it feels to be in this moment, in this location, seated in this deliberate posture. Take a minute now to welcome yourself to your practice, expressing your readiness to be present for yourself in this way.

3. Pay attention to your breathing. It's unnecessary to alter or influence the breath in any manner. Allow the breath to be exactly as it is at this moment. Simply follow the inhalation and exhalation of the breath.

4. Pay attention to where you are experiencing breath sensations. Maybe you can feel the air going in and out of your nose and upper lip. The mild stretching and contracting of the chest and ribs might be what you're feeling. Perhaps you're aware of your stomach rising and falling. Allow your focus to be drawn to the sensations of the breath as it enters and exits the body.

5. You may notice thoughts passing through your head while you sit here concentrating on your breath. There's no reason to shut out your ideas. Instead, check if you can let your thoughts travel through your head, one by one. Allow yourself to be free of the desire to categorize your ideas as good or bad, whether it's good or awful. Find a method to be with your ideas in a neutral way. Examine whether you can be aware of your ideas without holding or clinging to any one of them, without dismissing or denying any specific viewpoint.

6. At this point, pay attention to any sensations that may be present. Take a deep breath in and out. Recognize every emotion for what it is. We have feelings regarding our sentiments at times. One emotion may seem OK or acceptable while another does not. All emotions are welcome.

7. Now, pay attention to the sensations in your body. Warmth and coolness are both present. Tingling. Tightness. Pulsation. Relaxation. Hunger. Fullness. Take note of what's going on in your body right now. This should be done with patience and care. With curiosity, investigate both powerful and subtle feelings.

8. Check to see whether your posture has changed when you breathe in and out. Then, if necessary, make any modifications. Allow yourself to tune in to your body in its natural state.

9. Right now, focus solely on your breath. Follow three more full cycles of breathing as we reach the completion of this practice. Make every effort to be present for each one. Remember that because this location of awareness is inside you, you may access it at any time.

10. If you're ready, softly open your eyes if they've been closed. Prepare to reengage with the day by reacquainting yourself with your surroundings. Set an intention to bring awareness to everything you do and everyone you engage with.

Meditation on Loving-Kindness

1. Please choose a comfortable sitting or lying down posture. Allow your eyes to close, either completely or partially. Take a few deep breaths to ground yourself in your body and the current moment.

2. Place your palm over your heart, or wherever it seems safe and comfortable, as a reminder that you are bringing not just awareness but loving awareness to your experience and yourself.

3. Feel your breath where you notice it most readily after a time. Feel your body breathe in and out, and then observe the smooth movement of your breath again when your focus wanders.

4. Then, slowly relaxing your concentration on the breath, or continuing to be aware of your breath in the background, begin offering yourself words of love and compassion again and again... words that you need to hear, words that you can relish.

- *Please use sentences that are relevant to you if you already have them.*
- *If this is your first time meditating with phrases, please open your heart and mind to hear what you need to hear - wise and compassionate words that speak to you deeply.*

5. Repeatedly open your heart to these words and say them gently into your own ear. • Maybe you're hearing the words from the inside out, and they're resonating with you.

6. Allow the words to flood your being, even if only for this one instant. Refocus your attention if you sense your mind has wandered by sensing the feelings in your body. Return to your own body. Then you will realize how significant your words are. Come home to a welcoming environment.

7. Finally, let go of the sentences and relax in your own skin.

8. Gradually open your eyes.

Affectionate Breathing (18 min)

1. Please choose a comfortable posture in which your body will feel supported for the duration of the meditation. Then, softly close your eyes, either half or completely. Release any excess tension in your body by taking a few deep, relaxed breaths.

2. Place a palm over your heart or similarly relaxing area as a reminder that we're bringing not just awareness but compassionate awareness, to our breathing and ourselves. You may rest your hand or leave it there.

3. Now start to observe your breathing in your body, feeling yourself breathe in and out.

4. Simply allow your body to breathe you. You don't have to do anything. Perhaps note how the in-breath nourishes your body and the out-breath calms it.

5. Become aware of the rhythm of your breathing as it flows in and out. (pause) Allow yourself to become aware of the natural rhythm of your breathing.

6. Feel your entire body flow in sync with your breath, as if it were the sea.

• Like an inquisitive kid or a little dog, your thoughts will naturally wander. Simply return to the rhythm of your breathing when this happens.

• Allow your breathing to softly rock and caress your entire body, both externally and inside.

• If you choose, you may even give yourself up to your breathing, making it the only thing you think about. Taking on the form of the breath.

• Just take a deep breath. • Slowly and softly open your eyes. • Gently surrender your focus to the breath, resting quietly in your own experience, and letting yourself feel whatever you're experiencing and be just as you are.

Hey, are you enjoying the book? I'd love to hear your thoughts!

Many readers do not know how hard reviews are to come by, and how much they help an author

I would be incredibly grateful if you could take just 60 seconds to write a brief review on Amazon, even if it's just a few sentences!

Thank you for taking the time to share your thoughts!

Your review will genuinely make a difference for me and help gain exposure for my work.

Angela Wade

CONCLUSION

Congratulations! You've made it to the end.

I hope you've learned a lot from this book. Stress, anxiety, and other mental health conditions can be overwhelming, and this book aims to help you conquer these challenges by providing tips and strategies to self-regulate negative thoughts, emotions, and behaviors.

In the first part, we discussed what it means to be mentally ill and the negatives that can often be associated with that. We introduced cognitive restructuring and how you can shift your thinking from negative to more adaptive and rational perspectives. We then took an in-depth look at tackling depression and overcoming worry and anxiety through CBT.

In the second part, we discussed how to combat bipolar disorder using self-monitoring and other treatment options and how to use CBT techniques to tackle anger and poor sleep habits.

We finished the book off with some mindfulness-based cognitive therapy designed to enable more empathic awareness and to help better regulate emotions.

Throughout this book, you have learned activities and exercises that can be practiced over and over again. These are based on the latest CBT strategies and mindfulness.

Don't let your thoughts, emotions, moods, and behaviors overwhelm you, or keep you from realizing your goals and leading a happy, fulfilling life.

Whether you're new to CBT or you'd like to deepen your understanding, this book has everything you need.

Now that you have all the tools you need, don't hesitate to use them. You've got this!

If you enjoyed reading this book, please share your experience with others by leaving a review on Amazon.

Best wishes!

REFERENCES

Abiko, Y., Paudel, D., Matsuoka, H., Moriya, M., & Toyofuku, A. (2021). Psychological backgrounds of medically compromised patients and its implication in dentistry: A narrative review. *International Journal of Environmental Research and Public Health*, *18*(16), 8792. https://doi.org/10.3390/ijerph18168792

American Psychiatric Association. (n.d.). *DSM history*. Retrieved February 11, 2024, from https://www.psychiatry.org/psychiatrists/practice/dsm/about-dsm/history-of-the-dsm

Mead, E. (2023, September 22). How to benefit from mindful running & mindful exercise. *PositivePsychology.Com*. https://positivepsychology.com/mindful-running-exercise/

Cuncic, A. (2022, January 5). Questions to break the ice. *About Social Anxiety*. https://www.aboutsocialanxiety.com/questions-to-break-the-ice/

Dalton Associates. (n.d.). *Bipolar disorder: What is it, symptoms, and treatments*. Retrieved February 11, 2024, from https://www.daltonassociates.ca/conditions/bipolar-disorder/

Engler, J. (2022, April 26). *Jonah Engler Silberman on Mindfulness for Anxiety: A Guide for Beginners*. https://jonahenglerscholarship.com/jonah-engler-silberman-on-mindfulness-for-anxiety-a-guide-for-beginners/

Green, M. (2019). Inclusive library service to individuals with mental illnesses and disorders. *The International Journal of Information, Diversity, & Inclusion*, *4*(1), 119–126. https://doi.org/10.33137/ijidi.v4i1.32500

HarmonyHub. (2022, June 14). *what is self-compassion? The 3 laws.* Medium. https://medium.com/@HarmonyHub/what-is-self-compassion-the-3-laws-3656e88e219

Jantz, G. (2013, July 10). *You are not alone if you suffer from depression.* A Place of HOPE. https://www.aplaceofhope.com/you-are-not-alone-if-you-suffer-from-depression/

Johnson, D. W. (2019, June 5). Is it difficult to find solutions to problems that satisfy everyone involved? *Psychology Today*. https://www.psychologytoday.com/us/blog/constructive-controversy/201906/the-importance-taking-the-perspective-others

Kleinman, P. (2012). *Psych 101: Psychology facts, basics, statistics, tests, and more!* Adams Media. https://addspeaker.net/wp-content/uploads/2018/10/Psych-101-Paul-Kleinman.pdf

Langston, J. B. (2022). *The mental health CBT, DBT & act workbook (2 in 1): 101+ cognitive, dialectical & acceptance + commitment-based therapy skills for anxiety, depression, overthinking & mindfulness.* Johnathan B. Langston.

Legg, T. J., & Cherney, K. (2018, August 22). *Signs and symptoms of mild, moderate, and severe depression.* Healthline.

https://www.healthline.com/health/depression/mild-depression#severe-major-depression

McKenna, N. (2023, March 20). *What makes you an assertive person.* Medium. https://medium.com/@n.mckenna2020/what-makes-you-an-assertive-person-fcc27ed53142

Nathan, P., Correia, H., & Lim, L. (2004). *Panic stations! coping with panic attacks.* Centre for Clinical Interventions.

National Alliance on Mental Illness. (n.d.). *Listening to your body.* Retrieved February 12, 2024, from https://heartsandminds.nami.org/articles/listening-to-your-body/

National Alliance on Mental Illness. (2023). *Mental health by the numbers.* https://www.nami.org/mhstats

National Research Council, & Institute of Medicine. (2009). The etiology of depression. In *Depression in parents, parenting, and children: Opportunities to improve identification, treatment, and prevention.* National Academies Press (US). https://www.ncbi.nlm.nih.gov/books/NBK215119/

Rowe, S. (2021, September 14). *Distinguishing OCD from other conditions: Is it OCD or something else?* Psych Central. https://psychcentral.com/ocd/distinguishing-ocd-from-other-conditions?utm_source=ReadNext

Tucker-Ladd, C. (1996). Stress, trauma, anxiety, fears and psychosomatic. In *Psychological self-help.* The Self-Help

Foundation. https://www.psychologicalselfhelp.org/
Chapter5.pdf

University of Oklahoma Counseling Center. (n.d.). *Strategies for better sleep*. Retrieved February 12, 2024, from https://www.ou.edu/ucc/resources/sleep-troubl-sleep-hygiene

Wagner, J. B., Luyster, R. J., Tager-Flusberg, H., & Nelson, C. A. (2016). Greater pupil size in response to emotional faces as an early marker of social-communicative difficulties in infants at high risk for autism. *Infancy*, *21*(5), 560–581. https://doi.org/10.1111/infa.12128

Family Radio. (n.d.). *Navigating through emotions: Anger management*. Retrieved February 12, 2024, from https://familyradio316.com/navigating-through-emotions-anger-management/

12 types of meditation: which is the right one for you? (n.d.). *Level Supermind*. Retrieved February 11, 2024, from https://level.game/blogs/what-is-the-right-type-of-meditation-for-you?lang=en

Made in United States
Troutdale, OR
11/09/2024

24591525R00146